LAW SCHOOL 101

Survival Techniques from Pre-Law

to Being an Attorney

R. Stephanie Good
Attorney at Law

SPHINX® PUBLISHING
AN IMPRINT OF SOURCEBOOKS, INC.®
NAPERVILLE, ILLINOIS
www.SphinxLegal.com

First Edition, 2004

Published by: **Sphinx® Publishing, An Imprint of Sourcebooks, Inc.®**

<u>Naperville Office</u>
P.O. Box 4410
Naperville, Illinois 60567-4410
630-961-3900
Fax: 630-961-2168
www.sourcebooks.com
www.SphinxLegal.com/Sphinx

This publication is designed to provide accurate and authoritative information in regard to the subject matter covered. It is sold with the understanding that the publisher is not engaged in rendering legal, accounting, or other professional service. If legal advice or other expert assistance is required, the services of a competent professional person should be sought.
From a Declaration of Principles Jointly Adopted by a Committee of the American Bar Association and a Committee of Publishers and Associations

This product is not a substitute for legal advice.
Disclaimer required by Texas statutes.

Library of Congress Cataloging-in-Publication Data
Good, R. Stephanie.
  Law school 101 : survival techniques from pre-law to being an attorney / by R. Stephanie Good.-- 1st ed.
      p. cm.
  Includes index.
  ISBN 1-57248-374-1 (alk. paper)
  1. Law--Study and teaching--Law and legislation 2. Law students--United States--Handbooks, manuals, etc. I. Title: Law school one hundred one. II. Title: Law school one hundred and one. III. Title.
KF283.G66 2004
340'.071'173--dc22
                                    2004001923

Printed and bound in the United States of America.

BG — 10 9 8 7 6 5 4 3 2 1

Dedication

I dedicate this book to my brother, Jim Garrison. I know that you are watching over me and smiling with the pride that so often gave me my motivation for moving forward. You are deeply missed and greatly loved. My dream was yours first. Thus, this shining moment is devoted to you. Thank you for all that you were, all that you are, and all that you will always mean to me.

Acknowledgements

It is with sincere gratitude that I acknowledge all of the wonderful people who have helped to make this book a reality for me.

My husband, Ed, for your support and love and for allowing me the time and space to make this dream come true.

My sons, Brian and Christian—Brian, for your endless encouragement, wonderful advice (both legal and personal), and for contributing so much valuable information to this book. Christian, a.k.a. "Nether," for inspiring me with your persistence, your creativity, and your ability to overcome adversity.

My brother, Larry, for knowing how to open the doors that make dreams come true. Dad, for leaving me footsteps to follow in. Mom, for never doing my homework for me and instilling in me the belief that a woman can do anything. Emily, for your companionship and your ability to make me smile during the worst of times.

Austin, for your friendship and trust and for allowing me to help make a difference.

Karll, for the innumerable times that you came to my rescue at a moment's notice when my computers crashed

A special thank you to the people at Sphinx Publishing for believing in this book, especially Dianne Wheeler, Mike Bowen, and Christine Lock Garcia.

Another special thank you to my agent at Waterside Productions, Kimberly Valenti, for your tireless efforts in finding the perfect publishing company for *Law School 101*.

And finally, I want to express my gratitude to all the many legal eagles who opened their hearts and minds to contribute so much valuable input to this book.

God bless you all!

Contents

SECTION FOUR: SECOND YEAR

SECTION FIVE: CAREER CHASE

SECTION SIX: THIRD YEAR

SECTION SEVEN: AFTER SCHOOL

Introduction

You are at a party and people are standing around laughing loudly about something they all seem to agree upon. You inch closer and casually lean in to hear what they are saying. Someone blurts out, *What's the difference between a lawyer and a lobster?* Another, just as quickly replies, *One is a bottom-feeding, garbage-eating scavenger. The other is a fish.* Everyone bursts into hysterics, including you. However, deep inside you wonder why this kind of humor is so entertaining. Several thoughts run through your mind as a myriad of humorous punch lines resound in your ears. You think, *lawyers can't possibly be as conniving and deceitful as that stereotype being joked about. There must be something redeeming about them. After all, I'm thinking about applying to law school.*

Jokes about lawyers are rampant. Lawyers laugh along with others as insults are hurled their way only to hide their humiliation at being included in the harsh stereotype that has evolved over the years. The media portrays them as either dumb-blonde gorgeous or devil-possessed evil, while nighttime TV depicts them as conniving, money-hungry power-seekers who generally prevail at the expense of others. The lay person often views them as either snakes or members of an elite club comprised of people from another planet. Yet, in spite of all of the negative images, parents continue to encourage their children to apply to law school, seeing it as a way for them to ensure a secure future. Once accepted, many tend to think they are on the gravy train. Unfortunately, that is not always the case.

You are reading this book because you want to know the truth about the every-day life of a law student. Maybe you envision a school where intellectually stimulating conversations abound and highly-principled students spend their days enlightening each other with thought-provoking tidbits of profound knowledge. As the years pass, you imagine the students evolving into highly-skilled protectors of justice who hold court with interesting clients, litigate at exciting trials, drive sporty little foreign cars, escape to lavish country homes on weekends, and live in duplex townhouses near the office during the week. You imagine glorious dinner parties with colleagues, champagne toasts to victories, expense accounts, and a quick climb up the ladder of success.

But, you do have some doubts. You have heard stories and derogatory comments, such as *ambulance chaser* and *shark*, and you feel confused at being caught between your conflicting perceptions of two drastically different legal worlds. So, here you are, searching for guidance, seeking details that you have yet to find anywhere else. You need to know the truth, because your decision to apply to law school will be the single, most significant, life-altering commitment that you have ever made.

As you read through the following pages, you will soon realize that your search has ended. You have found the place where all your questions will finally be answered. By the time you finish reading this book, you will have a complete understanding of what law school and attorney-life are like. You will feel totally prepared to make an educated decision about whether or not to join the legal profession.

The purpose of this book is to furnish the tools that perspective law students need to survive in the law school environment and to thrive as attorneys. The main focus herein is not to teach you the law. You will have three years to learn that. This book will be your *pre*-law guide, so to speak, your survival tool. It will enlighten you to the rigorous existence that the student endures throughout the law school journey. You will be taken on a guided tour through the hallowed halls of legal indoctrination, from the decision-making process through all of the unexpected pitfalls and stresses of law school life. It will dispel your illusions and will encourage you to disregard what you have learned from television about the exciting and prosperous lives of law students and attorneys. It will impart a more accurate perception of what attending law school and practicing law is really like. Once you grasp how demanding the law school experience is, you are encouraged to take a serious inventory of your strengths and weaknesses so you can decide *prior* to entrance whether your expectations about meeting the challenges are realistic.

One thing should be kept in mind as you read through this book: the practice of law can be extremely rewarding. There is no better feeling than seeking a resolution to a client's problem and succeeding. Whether it be a situation that involves the possible incarceration of an innocent individual or a business deal that requires sharp negotiation skills, lawyers are necessary beings and there is little doubt that the world would be in chaos without them. They perform wonderful work and provide the most valuable of services.

This book was written from the heart. It is meant to alleviate a significant amount of the stress and disappointment that many future law students and attorneys will endure without the advice offered in the following chapters. My hope is that you will give serious thought to what you are reading *prior* to making the important decision to apply to law school. If you have already applied— the information will serve to help you adapt to the law school environment. If you are currently attending—this book will enable you to readjust your expectations of the legal profession prior to being sworn in as an attorney. If you are an attorney—this book will let you know that you are not alone in your struggle to survive in the profession.

The information provided in the following chapters is aimed directly at those people who share one common interest, someone's success in law school. No matter who you are or what you envision about attending law school, this book will change your views. Law school is serious business. It is a place where the stakes are high and the competition is fierce.

The material in this book has been broken into sections to better serve you. Starting with *Section One: Pre-Law*, information about examining your decision to go to law school is explored along with all the necessary preparatory work necessary to get into the school of your choice. *Section Two: First Year* walks you through the rite of passage from college graduate to first-year law student and gets you started on the right path. *Section Three: Knowing the Ropes Without Hanging Yourself* highlights study tips and shortcuts to make you a success. *Section Four: Second Year* outlines the transition to upper-class law students and identifies choices and opportunities available for the next two years. The next section, *Section Five: Career Chase*, explores the ins and outs of finding a legal related job and how to get it. *Section Six: Third Year* jumps right into the last year of law school where all thoughts turn to the bar exam. *Section Seven: After School* wraps up everything you have learned in law school and takes you from student to attorney-at-law.

Law school is truly about survival of the fittest and this book gives you all you need to know to survive in the fast-paced environment. Your experience does not have to be a disappointing one, if you go into it with eyes wide open and minds well-prepared.

SECTION 1

Pre-Law

*The future belongs to those who believe
in the beauty of their dreams.*
—Eleanor Roosevelt

chapter 1

Preparing for Law School

Thoughts to Ponder Before
Setting Foot on Hallowed Ground

You have finally arrived at law school. The buildings are historic and carefully constructed of sturdy, red bricks covered in centuries-old ivy. Tall, white columns elegantly frame each entranceway. The school is introduced to incoming students by sprawling, green blanketed lawns with dogwoods lining the walkways.

The salt and pepper-haired professors are distinguished gentlemen dressed in tweed cardigans with suede-patched sleeves. They grasp pipes tightly between their teeth and carry law books neatly tucked under their arms. They walk with their heads tilted at a thought- provoking angle, and as they quickly rush by, they lower their eyes, glance at you above their glasses, and smile curtly. You shyly grin back, turning your head with curiosity to catch a glimpse of who they are before they disappear into a swarm of new recruits.

You continue moving across campus along with the flowing current of eager students until you finally arrive at the school's main building, where an upper class person welcomes you with open arms, hands you your schedule, and escorts you to your first class. You quickly scour the room for a seat, eagerly looking around at all of the new friends you will make. Everyone is chattering away about their new endeavour and you avidly join in like an excited child. The professor enters, welcomes you, gives a brief description of the course, and sends you on your way with your first assignment. You search the building for your next class, which turns out to be a repeat of the last one.

In approximately one hour, your first day of law school comes to an end and you run off to meet some of your new friends for lunch. But, just as you approach the group, things become fuzzy. You begin to hear the distant sound of an alarm. It's getting louder and louder. You look around, scanning the parking lot to see if it's coming from someone's car. Your vision becomes even more distorted and you begin to feel light-headed. You try to continue across campus, but you feel as though you have lead in your legs. Just as panic sets in, you wake up.

• • • •

As pleasant as that experience was before the bells went off, unfortunately, your whole first day of school was nothing more than a dream. Hopefully, you will realize that *before* you get to law school, because if you are expecting your first day to be similar to that experience, you might want to go back to sleep and keep dreaming. Or, your more sensible option would be to read on and spend some time journeying into the *real world* of law.

If you are considering attending law school, your decision should not be entered into lightly. Those three years are going to force you to make life-altering changes. Your thought processes will forever be refurbished. Your perception of life will be turned upside down. Your friends and family will wonder what is happening to you. Law school is not like college, where you graduate excited about all of the ways to utilize your new-found knowledge. In law school, there is a direction in which you are travelling that will lead you down a very specific path. You will be indoctrinated into a world where the factual outweighs the theoretical, where reality smothers the imaginary, where the truth has to be sifted out from beneath all of the lies, where the good and bad seem to merge into a microcosm of uncertainty, and where you will be entrusted with the mission of sorting it all out and making some sense of it.

You need to be completely sure that this is the path that will ultimately take you home, that this is your true calling in life; because the commitment is huge and walking away is a difficult choice.

Do You Really Want to be an Attorney?

Prior to entering law school—in fact, even before you begin filling out your applications—take a serious look at your reasons for wanting to become an attorney. If your impression about being an attorney comes from what you have seen on shows like *Law and Order* and *The Practice*, you might want to do some further investigation. The truth is, weekly one-hour television series have very little time to present you with an accurate portrayal of what an attorney experiences on a day-to-day basis. You watch with excitement as crimes are committed, suspects are arrested, trials are held, and defendants are convicted—all within sixty minutes (including commercials). The end result is quick and painless, and you are left with the impression that the legal system is swift and stimulating, and that justice prevails most of the time.

In real life, arrests occur slowly, if ever. The commencement of a trial can take several months or longer, and the trial may last for weeks. Defendants are not always found guilty, and when they are, their punishments do not always satisfy their victims. It is time to come out of the world of make-believe and view what really goes on behind the doors of the legal world.

Law and Disorder

Practicing law is neither romantic nor, for the most part, exciting. It is a profession filled with paperwork, standing around courtrooms for hours on end, angry clients, antagonistic adversaries, overworked judges, dejected spouses, lonely kids, and yes, stress. It does have many good points, but not always as many as you would like. It can be very gratifying, but that may depend on whether or not you are practicing the type of law you really love or if you are stuck at a job because it is more lucrative than changing your focus. It may also depend on whether you generally prevail with your cases or if you are compatible with your colleagues. Whatever the case, as long as you are aware of and accept the realities of the profession, the practice of law can be a rewarding experience.

Too many people find their way into law school for the wrong reasons—under the misconception that becoming an attorney is romantic or that it will be their *ticket to ride*. They may have the feeling that they must move on with their lives and continue to better themselves after college. They have been taught that the legal profession is the key to making all of their dreams come true, whether it be for riches or status. However, most are unaware of what to expect, and once they arrive at law school, the realities are often difficult to endure. Yet, the commitment has already been made and the financial obligation has begun, which is why those who feel that they have made a mistake generally believe there is no other choice but to stay.

Most people enter the legal profession with sincere thoughts of honor, dignity, and a strong sense that they possess all the tools to move forward in their careers. However, they soon find that unpredictability and the law are synonymous. For example, you may arrive in court for an encounter with a client whom you have yet to meet, only to find that he has shown up for his arraignment on a drug charge wearing a hat with a marijuana leaf on it. Or, you may be greeted by a boy who shows up wearing suit pants and a t-shirt with a tuxedo shirt painted on. Courtroom decorum and individual style do not always go hand-in-hand. There are tattoos, nose rings, teased hair, low-cut blouses, muscle shirts, stretch pants, pink hair, shirts with obscenities, pants with holes, nasty attitudes, flirting floozies, angry parents, snotty girlfriends, and crass boyfriends who you will face with no advance warning. All of these characteristics belong to the individuals who may make up the vast array of people you will call clients.

In addition to quirky clients, you will be faced with arrogant judges, egotistical attorneys, power-hungry court officers, and many other eccentric entities that walk through the courthouse doors each and every day. There is no telling what you will find when you enter a courtroom looking for an adversary or, for that matter, your client.

EXHIBIT

An attorney was in the middle of zealously advocating to keep a female client out of jail, when she turned around in open court and, out of the blue, said to him, *Why don't you take that fat, ugly judge and shove him up your a—*. He stood there for a moment in total disbelief. After regrouping, he brazenly continued with his defense, trying to act as though nothing had happened. When he was finished speaking, there was complete silence—until the judge leaned forward, looked the defendant straight in the eye and said, *Young lady, I may be fat and I may be ugly, but this is my courtroom and if anyone is going to do the shoving, it'll be me!*

Yes, it happens. You may be dealing with some pretty shady clients and a few even stranger judges. At least you get used to the judges. But, with new clients coming and going, the predictability is, well, unpredictable!

Motivationally Speaking

Hopefully, by now, you are beginning to realize that there are some very important questions that you should be asking yourself in order to make an educated decision about applying to law school. Serious consideration must be given to why you really want to become an attorney and what you truly know about the profession before you begin such an important and tedious journey. You should do your best to determine your precise reasons for wanting to enter the legal world. That may seem like an easy quest to pursue.

However, once you begin meeting other future law students, you will be surprised to discover that there are many different motives for filling out law school applications.

For example, there are prospective law students who pursue a legal education because they have an idealistic view of the world and assume that they can make a difference for the rest of us.

EXHIBIT

A first-year student said that she was driven to apply to law school because she had always thought of herself as someone who could really change things. She wanted the world to be a better place, and since she was the type of person who volunteered for issues involved with social change, she thought that becoming an attorney was the next step along the road to saving the world. She also felt that her noble work would help to improve the negative image that a lot of attorneys have garnered.

On the other hand, perhaps your motive is money. Maybe you think that becoming an attorney ensures you expensive cars and estate-like homes.

EXHIBIT

Another fairly new law student said that he was driven by the thought of making a lot of money. He had always wanted to become an attorney, mostly because he envisioned the profession as one where he would be retained by high profile clients whose fees would make him very wealthy. He wanted to earn as much money as he could and retire a very rich man.

Power is another incentive. As an attorney, you will most definitely be in a position of power since someone else's problems become yours to solve.

EXHIBIT

A second-year student said that he thought of attorneys as power brokers, people who hold others' lives in their hands. He said that he wanted to be able to have the influence to make decisions about important matters involving the law. His initial plan included getting involved in local politics.

Some of the most disenchanted students are those who entered law school because family members had expected them to attend. They had been pressured to follow in the footsteps of a relative and it had never occurred to anyone, including the student, that it was the furthest thing from his or her mind.

EXHIBIT

A third-year student was struggling with the idea of spending the rest of his life in the profession of law. He had always known that he would someday attend law school, mainly because nothing else was ever discussed in his home. His grandfather was an attorney, as was his father and older brother. It was just something that was expected of him, and he never even considered the possibility of not going.

But now, nearing the end of school, after holding a couple of legal jobs and participating in a clinical program, he felt somewhat disappointed with the whole process. He said that there were so many other things that he now realized he would have been much better suited for, but due to his financial investment, as well as his family's expectations, he felt trapped.

Whatever factors lead you to consider attending law school, you must arrive at the decision based on sound reasoning, because once you make the commitment, it is very hard to walk away. If attending law school is not your own idea, please think long and hard before applying. It is difficult enough to survive in the environment when you have your heart set on it. Attending at the insistence of someone else only makes the possibility of excelling less probable. If it *is* your idea, but you have the notion that an attorney's life is somewhat akin to what you have viewed on *Law and Order* or *The Practice*, you might also want to rethink your decision.

Take Inventory

In order to feel confident that you are applying to law school for the appropriate reasons, take a serious inventory of your thoughts on the subject. Write out your reasons and analyze whether they are realistic based on what you have learned first-hand about lawyers and law school, and not what you imagine it to be like from what you saw on some weekly prime-time show.

Begin by asking yourself the following questions.

Do I think that I can save the world?

Do not expect to save the world. Recent reports state that it takes a village just to save one small child. However, in the words of the late anthropologist, Margaret Mead, *Never believe that a few people can't change the world. For indeed, that's all who ever have.*

Am I applying because I believe that it will make me rich?

It depends on how you define the word *rich*. Everybody's view is different. Just remember these words: *The real measure of your wealth is how much you'd be worth if you lost all your money.*

Do I view being an attorney as holding a powerful position?

Power is overrated. If that is what you need to feel good about yourself, get some counselling before you attend law school.

And, as Abraham Lincoln said, *Nearly all men can stand adversity, but if you want to test a man's character, give him power.*

Am I applying because my family is pressuring me to go?

Unless your family members have a prearranged plan to attend school for you, complete all of your assignments, and take your exams (including the bar), do not let them influence your decision. Sir Walter Scott clearly agreed with that thought when he said, *All men who have turned out worth anything, have had the chief hand in their own education.*

Do I believe that the legal profession is exciting?

If you do, turn off your television and go sit in a courtroom for a few days. Just think of the words of former United States Supreme Court Justice Warren Burger when he commented, *Ours is a sick profession. [A profession marked by] incompetence, lack of training, misconduct and bad manners. Ineptness, bungling, malpractice, and bad ethics can be observed in courthouses all over this country every day.*

Will I be happy if I end up with a job that was not in my original plan?

Hmm...good question, however, you are the only one who can make this decision. But, as E. M. Forster so eloquently stated, *We must be able to let go of the life we have planned, so as to have the life that is waiting for us.*

These questions and thoughts are just the beginning. There are many more to ask, but for now, start with the basics. Try to determine what is going through your mind about applying to law school. The best way to do that is to continue moving forward, questioning your motives until you are sure of what you truly want to do and why you want to do it.

Consider doing the following:

- Write down all of the reasons why you want to go to law school.
- Visit a law school and walk around to get a feel for the environment.
- Talk to some of the students to understand their impressions.
- Arrange a meeting with a law school counselor to discuss your concerns.
- Ask for permission to sit in on a few classes.
- Ask for a syllabus to get an idea of the workload.
- When you get home, go over your list of reasons for attending and see if any of them have changed. This is the time to determine which one of your reasons for attending is the most realistic and which may not be valid anymore.

Applying to law school is a decision that must come from your inner being. It should spring from a burning desire that reaches down to the depths of your soul, something that you instinctively know is right for you. Law school is rigorous and stressful, and only those people who have a genuine ambition to become an attorney and are fully aware of what they will experience are likely to survive and actually enjoy themselves.

Lifelines

Since you have already begun the process of figuring out what your motives are for applying to law school, it is now a wise idea to take a close look at your life situation to see if you are equipped to handle the next three years. Life situations can, and most certainly will, interfere with law school. Difficult relationships, marriages, jobs, children, illnesses, family emergencies or demands, money problems, and many other issues will add to the stress that can make your time at law school less than perfect. Advanced preparation for all of your arduous law school moments will help you survive the ordeal.

Ponder the following questions before beginning your upcoming journey.

Are you financially secure or will you be able to obtain enough financial aid to support yourself for at least the first year?
Law schools generally recommend that you do not seek outside employment during your first year. The workload is extremely heavy and somewhat confusing. It takes all of the time you have and more just to stay on top of your assignments. If you think you can slide through and cram at the end, you will not succeed.

EXHIBIT

An attorney who had been out of school for a few years told me that the biggest mistake he made was working during his first year, just as he had through college. He was under the impression that college life and law school life would be synonymous. After a few months had gone by, he realized that he was not keeping up with his course load and his grades showed it.

Are you able to be disciplined and structured without anyone else's guidance?
Good organizational skills are essential in order to achieve success in law school. Even if you excelled in college, you will now need to evaluate your ability to be self-disciplined in a way that you have yet been required to do. Unlike college, where there are several ways to determine how you are doing throughout a course, law school grades most often depend on one, end-of-the-semester final exam or paper. These types of exams and papers are not like those you crammed for or threw together at the last minute in college. Your ability to stay on top of your work all along, and to begin researching and writing papers as soon as assignments are given, is essential for law school success.

It is important to note that your grades are completely dependent upon how well those around you perform. Therefore, it is not enough to do bare bones work. You must study harder than you think possible. You must continuously review your notes, outline them, and try to fully understand the doctrines that you are taught. What your professors are looking for is your ability to understand concepts and policy issues and to analyze facts and determine their significance in relation to laws, rather than to merely regurgitate memorized assignments back as you may have in college. Your goal is to take a situation, analyze it, apply the law, and come to a reasonable conclusion. This will be your introduction to the way that you will practice law. Then, in the future, when you find yourself reading a case or a statute, analyzing and applying a rule of law to a set of facts, or writing a memorandum, you will possess the necessary tools to dissect and examine the circumstances and predict some type of reasonable outcome.

In law school, even if you do not keep up with your readings, you will still be expected to think on your feet and argue your position in an intelligible manner when called on. Do not assume that you are going to slide through and succeed at the highest level with the same amount of effort that you relied on in college. Self-discipline and hard work are essential ingredients, and without them, you are not likely to survive law school.

Do you have a support system to fall back on when the going gets rough?

A good support system can make all the difference when you are under the gun. The stress will overtake you if you are not able to rely on those closest to you to be supportive and synergistic during your three difficult years at school. You may be living on campus and need someone back at home to help keep things under control for you, such as bills, friendships, and even relationships. If you can confine your focus only to your studies, it will help ease the pressure. Or, when taking exams or trying to make the deadline on a paper, you might just need to blow off some steam to someone who really knows you. That is when those at home are most essential to your survival.

EXHIBIT

A young attorney said that he had a very difficult time trying to juggle a job, law school, and life in general. He found himself calling home late at night just to hear a familiar voice. He said that it centered him to know that in the end, there was still an anchor in his life who understood him. It was that stronghold that helped him to keep his head together during those late night anxiety attacks.

Are your personal relationships strong enough to survive your commitment to law school?

It is not uncommon for couples to break up while one partner is attending law school. Even if their relationship survived college, something dramatic happens when one enters law school. It is easy to misinterpret all of the long hours of schoolwork as an unfaithful or neglectful partner. It is also difficult for the law school partner to have nobody to come home to who truly understands or relates to him or her. The significant other often does not accept the fact that law school is so much more demanding than college. He or she may feel rejected and challenge the stories of hard work and stress offered as an explanation for the inattention. Unfortunately, when that happens, many of those relationships *crash and burn* as law students often turn to each other for the understanding and support that they crave.

Not all relationships take a nosedive. The strong and steadfast, the trusting ones, the well-prepared couples who understand and are willing to accept the ups and downs of law school, and those with the most common bonds, will all have the best chance to survive the challenges without feeling threatened. It is all about knowing ahead of time what to expect and figuring out a plan to deal with it.

If your relationship is not on solid ground, be prepared to end it. But, do not despair, you may say good-bye to an old relationship and hello to your future spouse at law school.

Do you know how to handle stress?

Stressing out never made a situation easier. It never got you a higher grade or a better job. It never solved a problem for you. It is a useless waste of energy. Things will get done and you will finish your tasks. The better able you are to deal with stress, the more likely it is that things will turn out fine. So, take a good look at your life and at your past ability to deal with tense situations. If you are the type of person who cracks under pressure, you might want to reconsider your decision to apply to law school. On the other hand, if you think that you can change your pattern of caving in from stress, perhaps some anxiety-reduction techniques will allow you to move forward comfortably. The best way to handle the pressure of a tense situation is to take a deep breath and keep reminding yourself of the following things.

- You chose to be there.
- Everyone else feels the same way as you.
- A clear head will help you to prevail.

Can you withstand humiliation?

To survive law school, you need a strong backbone and a thick skin. You must be able to take criticism and, at times, some berating. It comes with the territory. If you are too full of yourself to be humble or too sensitive to be verbally assaulted in front of a roomful of fellow students, you will not survive law school or the practice of law. However, it is important to note that everyone gets the same dose of *degradation*. So, when it is your turn, if you can roll with the punches, you will get along very well. And, remember, while you may not understand this yet, for the most part, there are valid reasons behind the harsh treatment.

Do you possess the necessary skills to succeed in law school?

Law school will help to prepare you for the legal world, but it will only do so by polishing and refining your current skills, not by creating new ones where none exist. By the time you set foot into law school, you have already gone through college and you should be well aware of where your strengths and weaknesses lie. You know if your papers were unacceptable or your oral presentations were less than adequate. Maybe you were unable to organize yourself enough to pass muster or you could not see past black and white on an issue to look at all of the extenuating circumstances. That is not to say that there is absolutely no hope for you, but you will be hit hard with reality when you are up against people who have skills far exceeding those within your own realm.

If you do not possess analytical skills, problem solving abilities, research and writing skills, solid oral communication skills, sound organization skills, the ability to follow instructions, to think outside the box, to demonstrate care and concern for your fellow human beings, to accept defeat and move on, and to gracefully achieve victory, then you will have a very difficult time surviving law school and the legal profession.

Are you a good judge of character?

An attorney often needs to possess the perception of an eagle, because reading people is an essential ingredient to success in the legal world. For example, a trial attorney needs to understand human nature in order to pick an adequate jury for his or her case to prevail. Sometimes, it is not the initial questioning of a juror that is important. The right juror may be chosen, in part, based upon answers given during *voir dire* (the jury questioning period), and, in part, due to character traits that may have special meaning to an observant attorney.

EXHIBIT

A seasoned trial attorney says that she often watches jurors carefully before making her selection. She knows how to pick out certain details that give her insight into what people are really like before talking to them. She looks at things such as the book they carry, the newspaper they read, the way they wear their hair, and the type of clothes they have on in order to get a read on how they might vote on the jury.

The same holds true while listening to a perspective juror's answers. Often, an attorney must be perceptive enough to read between the lines to get the real scoop on how a person might vote on a jury. If someone feels strongly enough about an issue, their opinions can cloud their judgement to be fair and impartial.

An attorney must also be able to discern a client's character. You do not want to take on the case of someone you will not feel completely comfortable representing. You may be conducting business meetings, drawing up contracts or a commercial lease, creating estate planning documents, representing an alleged criminal, and doing a whole host of other tasks for people; you need to know you can work with them. Your accurate perception of others must be your guiding force.

Sense and Sensibility

There is an impression afloat that if you are not able to tear someone to shreds on the witness stand, you will be a failure as an attorney. So, let's think about that. First of all, many attorneys never set foot into a courtroom and never have the opportunity to question witnesses. But, for those who do—there is something to be said for keeping a witness on his or her toes, there is also something to be said for thoughtful and crafty questioning.

It is not only about the manner in which you say something. What you have to say is just as important if not even more significant. If you are going to corner a witness, all the badgering in the world will be useless without the competency to ask the pertinent questions. The same thing applies in any area of law that you practice, even if your task is to negotiate an effective contract. There is a definite need for patience and professionalism, not a *great white*. Whatever you have heard about the correlation between man-eating sharks and successful attorneys should be put to rest.

While for the most part, in a court case, only the evidence is supposed to carry weight, jurors are human and they do get *vibes* from people. Unfortunately, those vibes can sometimes make them vote a certain way that might not necessarily make sense to a bystander or fall within the scope of the guidelines that are given by a judge.

It is easy to imagine this type of thing happening when you think about how the demeanor of a defendant influences a juror depending upon how credible he or she appears. Sometimes, especially in cases that rely heavily on circumstantial evidence, the believability of a person is the deciding factor, and even attorneys and the way they handle themselves can be taken into account.

A juror may see an attorney and be reminded of somebody he or she dislikes. It might be due to something as simple as the way an attorney walks or smiles or the cologne he or she wears. If it rubs a juror the wrong way, there is no telling how it could sway the way he or she votes. That is not to say that a juror sits in the deliberation room and says, *I don't like the way Mr. Jones walked over to the defense table. I will find his client guilty.* But subconscious thoughts about people often surface to influence our decisions about matters not at all related to those thoughts.

An overbearing or ineffectual personality can make all the difference to someone who is in the position of determining the outcome of your case. If there is something that you are aware of about yourself that might offend or alienate others more often than you care to admit, you should attempt to rectify the situation.

The point being imparted upon you is that your personality can make a difference in the way that your cases will go, the type of clients that will be drawn to you, and the way other members of the legal community accept you as one of their own. Whether you are negotiating a contract, trying a case, mediating a marital dispute, or drafting a will, who you are must be consistent with the objectives that this profession clearly warrants. Take a good, hard look at the type of human being that you are, the way you handle different situations (especially stressful ones), and the things that excite you the most about the legal profession. Making the right choice about the line of work that interests you is essential no matter what profession you choose to enter.

Whatever the story, whatever the profession, you must be content with what you are doing in life. In the legal profession, there are many areas for you to practice in, depending on your ambitions. The only comment that bears serious thought about whether or not your personality should keep you from considering the practice of law is if you are so wishy-washy that you have a difficult time speaking up for yourself and others, and you find it impossible to take a position on an issue. Otherwise, unless you are just the type of person who tends to turn people off, your personality, in and of itself, should not keep you out of law school. You may be quite laid back and be an excellent litigator. Or, you may never set foot into a courtroom at all and practice an area of law that keeps you behind a desk. Either way, it would be wise to research all aspects of the practice of law to see if and where you might fit in prior to making the commitment.

Returning to School Later in Life

Law schools are seeing more and more returning, older students, whose lives have come to a point where they are inspired to finally fulfill a long-awaited dream to become an attorney. Due to the special nature of those students and their often unique ability to adjust to difficult situations easier than those with less life experience, they often succeed in law school and handle the pressures better.

Contrary to popular belief, there are many advantages to being an older student. Life experience teaches us that survival is possible in even the most arduous conditions. Older students usually return to school knowing exactly what they hope to accomplish. They have a plan and they are driven to reach their goals. Unlike many younger students, they are not interested in what is happening on Saturday night or what the coolest clothes are this season. They understand the seriousness of making an expensive commitment and they use their well-earned survival skills to overcome tough situations. They know only too well that living through difficult times usually results in shaping us into better human beings. Thus, they face it head on and work through it.

EXHIBIT

A woman who entered law school at the age of thirty-eight said that when her friends heard about her plans, they made jokes about why she was really going, saying that she must be having a mid-life crisis. They also quipped that she would be forty-one upon graduation and much too old to start out in a new profession. Nobody took her decision seriously. They thought she was crazy to begin such a life-changing experience at her age. Her response was perfect. She declared, *I'm going to be forty-one in three years no matter what I'm doing. So, I can either continue sitting around the house waiting for the kids to return from school or I can embark upon a new and exciting career challenge.*

There is a sense of rebirth for older students who return to the classroom. It is a wonderful way to challenge your mind again.

While being older or having more life experience may be an advantage, it can also bring with it some complicated baggage.

EXHIBIT

A second-year student who was older than most of her class-mates entered law school with two small children at home. Due to the many circumstances of motherhood and her lack of understanding about what she was getting herself into, she was barely able to compete with students who lived on campus and had all the time in the world to study in the library. She stuck it out because she had already made a huge financial commit-ment, but she said that both her children and her schoolwork suffered for her efforts.

Just as with any other law school applicant, older students must be fully aware of what to expect upon entering law school. You should take the opportunity to evaluate all of the pros and cons prior to making the commitment to determine whether or not it is right for you. Just keep in mind all of the many great advantages of being an older student.

While it is not an easy commitment for anyone to make, older students do find themselves somewhat better able to cope with what may appear to a younger person to be unimaginable obstacles. It is generally true that older students have overcome many stumbling blocks and come to the point in life where they somehow manage to prioritize what to stress out about. While there will still be many anxiety-ridden moments no matter who you are, an older student has probably been through much worse than school, and will hopefully face the angst with a somewhat more positive attitude than younger students. Either way, as with the younger students, older ones need to possess all of the tools to take the uncertainty and anxiety out of the law school experience. Law school can be a wonderful world and it should not be passed up merely because of your age.

chapter 2

Applying to Law School

The Paper Chase Commences

So, you are still serious about going to law school. Well, in order to get in, you must apply. The process for applying is not that far removed from what you experienced when you decided to go to college. You have to do an enormous amount of investigation to decide not only which law schools you want to apply to, but also which ones will actually consider you for acceptance. Part of that process involves beginning your research about law schools as early as the end of your junior year of college.

An excellent resource to aid in your search for law schools is the Internet Legal Resources Guide at **www.ilrg.com/rankings.html**. This site provides links to information regarding law school profiles, tuition, student to faculty ratio, admissions information, statistics, Bar pass rates, employment rates after graduation, and various other resources important to your investigation.

Personal Essay

Your law school application will consist of several items, including your personal essay, letters of recommendation, and copies of your college transcripts. When writing your personal essay, consider it your opportunity to demonstrate those qualities that will make you a good candidate for law school. Write about your goals in life, your reasons for wanting to pursue a legal career, and what attributes make you more desirable than other candidates. Additionally, your personal essay is a chance for admissions committees to view your writing skills. Your ability to frame your essay thoughtfully and proficiently will demonstrate the most important quality that you will bring with you to law school: your writing ability. Excellent writing skills are crucial to your success, not only on exams and papers, but also in your practice of law.

Letters of Recommendation

Letters of recommendation are an admissions committee's way of hearing about your attributes from an outside source. You should choose who writes them for you very carefully. Make sure the person is someone who knows you well and can speak about your strengths in a positive manner. It is preferable that your letters of recommendation come from those in an academic setting. However, that depends on how long it has been since you graduated from college. If a few years have passed, letters from recent employers would serve you just as well.

GPA

After receiving your application materials, the *Law School Data Assembly Service* (LSDAS) (a service almost all law schools require their applicants to register with) calculates a new LSDAS GPA (grade point average) for you using every grade that you received as part of your undergraduate degree. All GPAs from any school attended will be computed into your new LSDAS GPA. Then they will then take that new GPA, along with the other materials in your application package, and send them to each of the law schools to which you have applied.

Putting it all Together

In addition to **www.ilrg.com/rankings.html**, most law schools offer information on their requirements, including median *LSAT* (Law School Admission Test) scores, GPAs, and the percentile of students admitted who fall within your range. You can generally request that they mail it to you, along with their application packages, catalogues, and any other materials that are of interest to you. You may also be able to access it on their websites, along with the necessary downloads to make applying simple and swift.

Furthermore, your college will most likely be able to provide you with guidance regarding law schools, their requirements, and application materials. The vast array of information available to you will make choosing the right law school an easy process. For example, on the Internet Legal Resource Guide website, you are able to compare tuition rates to help you determine which schools are accessible to you financially. Your financial situation is one thing that must be kept at the forefront of your decision-making process. You should make every effort to determine which schools are within your reach financially, whether it be from out-of-pocket funds, financial aid, or scholarship money. You might find it surprising that the schools that rank in the top tier are not necessarily the most expensive to attend. For instance, Florida State University, which ranks number sixty-four in the U.S.News and World Report rankings for the top one hundred law schools, ranks number twelve for cost of tuition, with number one being the most expensive. This means that many of the top-tiered schools that you might think would be out of your reach financially, actually cost less than some of the schools that you are leaning towards due to your financial status. Some other factors that may influence your decision to attend a particular school are Bar pass rates and employment rates after graduation.

Play the Field

When applying, no matter how exceptional your credentials are, always play it safe by sending at least a couple of applications to schools that you know are definitely within your GPA range of acceptance. In the same vein, send a couple to those you think might be out of your reach. Since you will most likely be sending out applications prior to receiving your LSAT score (discussed in further detail later), it is important to not limit your range of law schools by only applying to those of a certain rank. Never set your sights so low that you miss out on an opportunity to achieve something you thought impossible. But keep your expectations realistic and do not allow yourself to lose hope if you do not get into one of the top-tiered law schools. Allow yourself to play the field a little bit.

Aside from your credentials, choosing the right school may involve many other factors, including where you want to practice law. This is an important issue to consider, because your law school career counseling center will frequently offer you access to employment opportunities aimed at listings in the general locale of the school. Law firms often post job listings with schools in their areas, unless they are top-tier firms who list with top-tier schools whose students are known to relocate where the money is. You may be on your own when looking for a job away from where your law school is known.

College Majors

There are a number of details that will impress law school admissions committees, including an excellent LSAT and a strong GPA. Other issues strongly considered are life experiences, as well as whether or not an applicant is a minority, a returning student, handicapped, or has some unique history that sets them apart from the rest.

However when it comes to your college major there is no reason to believe—as many prospective law students do—that having focused on physical education or art will eliminate or greatly reduce your chances of attending law school. The fact is, those majors stand out and make admissions committees take notice. That is not to say that a political science or pre-law major will not be accepted. But, when considering applicants, law schools tend to focus strongly on what makes you different rather than what makes you stand on common ground with everyone else. After all, if they have four hundred applications in front of them and only one hundred openings, and three hundred and ninety are from people who majored in the same area of concentration, they will move on to attributes that will differentiate one from the crowd.

School Rank

It makes sense that law schools prefer to admit students who will raise the bar on their institutions. They seek independent thinkers and people who do not necessarily follow along with the masses. While a non-law related major is helpful, the weight it will be given depends on certain factors.

For instance, if you have an easy major from a less than challenging educational institution, you will not impress the committee. If you have a difficult major from that same institution and someone with the same major from a more impressive university has applied, again, you will not fare as well. The more formidable the school, the more notice will be taken.

The college's reputation has everything to do with the way that your grades will be evaluated. If your school is in the competitive range and you did well, do not despair just because you focused on physical education or theatre. It may be your ticket into law school, after all. And if your college is not way up there, your major may give you the added push to make the law school admissions committee take notice.

One other point to consider is the status of the law school to which you are applying. Law school rankings are readily available at various places, including online at **www.usnews.com/usnews/ edu/grad/rankings/law/brief/lawrank_brief.php**. If the school of your choice ranks as one of the top-tiered (top twenty-five) law schools in the country and your LSAT scores and GPA are average or below, your application will not be seriously considered. Those schools are inundated with applications that generally come from students who attended top-tiered colleges. For the handful of seats that they have available, they are quite selective about who will be admitted. So do not set yourself up for rejection by only applying to Yale and Harvard if your scores are not way up within their zone of approval.

Keep in mind that there may be other extenuating factors that might make them consider you, even though those factors must be outstanding to overcome lower scores. For instance, if there are valid reasons why your GPA might not reflect your true potential, you can make that known in your personal statement. However, it would be helpful if a downward spiral in grades on your college transcript is a brief one and there are higher grades that reflect your true capabilities. Recommendations from professors who can help to put your transcript into the proper perspective will also be beneficial.

Know the Process

To avoid the disappointments that many students encounter, it would be wise for you to meet with counselors at your college or take the time to perform the previously recommended online research to try and determine which law schools admit students with your credentials. You do not want to waste money and time applying to schools that are clearly out of your reach.

Exhibit

A newly-admitted law student said that her experience with rejections was extremely frustrating. She had good grades from a *half-way decent college* and her LSAT score was also *pretty good*. So, when she was rejected from schools like Colombia, New York University, and Fordham, she was devastated. She had no idea about the selection process and the stiff competition. She had applied to excellent law schools thinking that she would have no problem being accepted, and unfortunately, it took all of those rejections to make her realize that she was setting her sights too high.

Transferring In

If you are intent on attending a particular law school, another option would be to transfer there after your first year, if you have excelled enough academically. While it is not a highly recommended path to take, it can work for you if you have valid reasons for wanting to be at a better school. If it is just something you want to do because the name of the school is more prestigious, transferring is a waste of time. If you have high aspirations about where you want to work—i.e., only as a judge's law clerk or at top-level law firms—and you believe that you have the ability to excel at a higher rated school, go for it. If the law school of your choice is in a location that makes your life much easier to cope with and you can gain entrance through transferral, do it. If you are at a school that focuses mainly on preparing students to pass the bar exam of that particular state, but you will be practicing law in another, transferring may be the best way to go. If you are attending a school that focuses on federal law and you would rather study at an institution that gears their program towards helping you to prepare for practicing in that state, you also have a valid reason to transfer.

However, keep in mind that you are going to spend three years in law school and your first, generally being the most stress-filled, is when you form your strongest bonds with other students. During your first year, you will be moving from one class to another with the same people every day, while learning all the ropes of survival in that particular school. You will be meeting professors and becoming familiar with their policies regarding grading and class participation, which are helpful when choosing your courses during your second and third years. Thus, there is something to be said for staying put. Moreover, if you transfer into a new school at the beginning of your second year, you may be greatly reducing your chances of being invited to join the prestigious law review journal or the other almost equally impressive journals that may prove to be your ticket to get that high paying job later on. Thus, your motive for transferring to a higher rated school is to get a better job, you just might be sabotaging yourself. That said, those factors may not influence you to remain where you are, especially if you have your heart set on seeing a particular law school's name inscribed on your diploma.

What's in a Name?

No matter which schools you choose to apply to, the education you receive will generally be sufficient to start you off in the practice of law. While some schools have better reputations than others, lower-tiered schools churn out some extremely well-respected, successful attorneys. So keep in mind while filling out your applications, that aside from the so-called prestigious law firm that is willing to pay you top-dollar to work your life away, the name of your law school is no indication of your future potential for becoming a successful attorney.

The LSAT

As the name implies, the *Law School Admissions Test*, or *LSAT*, as it is commonly called, is the test that every potential law student must take. There is no question that when law school admissions committees review applications, your LSAT score is the most important item in your entire package. The higher your score, the more desirable you are.

The LSAT, administered four times a year in February, June, October, and December, is the required exam for admittance to all law schools belonging to the *Law School Admission Council* (LSAC), a nonprofit corporation whose main responsibility it is to administer the exam.

While you may register for the exam by phone or mail, **www.LSAC.org** offers online registration. The website also provides a wealth of information to assist you in not only applying for the LSAT, but guiding you every step of the way. They provide many pre-law resources, including help with LSAT preparation, various tools for applying to law school, links to law school websites that may even enable you to take virtual tours, financial aid resources, downloadable forms, and numerous other valuable links to help answer many of your questions regarding entrance to law school.

The LSAT is a half-day, multiple-choice exam consisting of five, thirty-five minute sections and one thirty minute writing sample. It is graded on a scale of 120 to 180, with 180 being the highest. Only four of the five sections actually count towards the applicant's score. Although the writing sample is not graded, it is still sent to all of the schools to which the applicant applies.

Comparing applicants' LSAT scores is the principal way that an admissions committee determines who stands above the rest. Even a lower college GPA can be overshadowed by an outstanding LSAT score. However, while it may seem a necessary ingredient for determining success in law school, some do not necessarily view it as accurate a tool as one might assume.

Exhibit

A third-year law student said he was completely disillusioned after receiving his LSAT score. He was not a strong standardized test taker and had not performed well on the exam. In spite of his outstanding achievements in college, his less than admirable LSAT score resulted in him not being accepted into the law school of his choice. He considered not attending at all, but had a change of heart when remembering his experience with the SATs. He had not performed well on those either, yet he still made it to the top five percent of his college class. So, with some hesitation, he entered law school. He soon found himself excelling in all of his classes. He is about to graduate in the top ten percent with a nice job waiting for him after graduation.

Just as there are preparatory courses for other important exams, there are courses of instruction to ready you for the LSAT. It is highly recommended that you attend one and use the readily available practice exams as much as possible.

If you do not fare well the first time around, the LSAT can be retaken to obtain a higher score. Depending on the school that you apply to, they may accept the better grade or they may average the two. Another advantage that you have regarding a mediocre score is that if you leave the exam knowing that you bombed, you may immediately, or by written notification within five days of the exam, cancel your score. The fact that you cancelled will be noted on your score report, but it may not make a difference to anyone reviewing your application materials. It is wise to try to schedule your exam at the earliest possible juncture in order to allow for more than one sitting, just in case a second test becomes necessary. But be careful not to cancel your score too hastily, as the stress of the exam situation may lead you to underestimate what could turn out to be an impressive score.

Once you have taken the exam, the *Law School Data Assembly Service* (LSDAS) will take your score, along with your other application materials, consisting of your personal essay, letters of recommendation, and copies of your college transcripts, and send them out to your chosen law schools. This is the beginning of the process that takes you on the long road to becoming an attorney.

Summer Solstice

You have spent a lot of time learning about getting into law school. Another important aspect that will help to ease you into the process is how you spend your last nonlaw school moments. What you do with your time during those few short months just prior to entering law school is essential to your ability to handle the enormous workload that you are about to encounter.

There are many stories about the type of advice that pre-law students receive regarding how to properly prepare for their transition to law school. One thing that always seems to come up is what to do during the summer before the commencement of classes.

There are suggestions about various law books to read, courses to take, people to meet, and legal jobs to obtain. My initial thought about all of that is simple: you are about to embark on a long and difficult journey; taking the above suggestions would be comparable to jogging ten miles just to warm up on the morning of your first marathon.

Most new students arrive at law school during the month of August following their spring graduation from college. They have spent the past seventeen years sitting at desks, learning lessons, asking questions, answering questions, hearing lectures, doing homework, writing papers, and taking exams. While there is something to be said for performing a great deal of preparation prior to entering law school, there is one thing that you do not need to do—more work!

You *do not need to read a stack of law books* just so you can try to get ahead of all of the other students who, along with you, will most likely be completely bewildered throughout most of their first year. Reading a law book without anyone to explain the legalese is like picking up a Spanish book and attempting to understand it without having learned the language.

You *do not need to sit in a classroom taking law courses*. You will have three years to do that. I took a Constitutional Law class in college and, other than introducing me to the Constitution, it did absolutely nothing to prepare me for the law school course of the same name.

With that being said, there are programs designed to prepare you for the law school experience. One such course is the *BarBri Law School Prep Course*. It is a five day immersion program taught by *real* law professors and designed to ensure that students going to law school *really* want to go. It also provides strategies and insights needed for success in addition to those you will learn in this book. You can get more information at **www.lawschoolprep.com**.

Meeting with an attorney may not be a bad idea prior to making your decision to attend. You might be greatly influenced by listening to an attorney's perspective. But once you have made the commitment to attend law school, go talk to your friends, because you will not be hanging out with them very much after classes begin.

Do you really want to spend your last nonlaw school summer *working in a law firm?* I think you might have more fun working as a bartender, a lifeguard, or a tour guide, because beginning next summer, you will probably be spending the rest of your life working in law firms.

The truth is, you do not need to learn the law in advance to survive law school. You need to learn *survival techniques*. Prior to diving into the pool, you learn about water safety. Prior to getting behind the wheel of a car, you learn about the rules of the road. Prior to going to law school, you need to learn how to survive in the competitive and stressful environment. Once you can do that, learning the law will fall into place.

SECTION 2

First Year

It is not the strongest of the species that survive, nor the most intelligent, but the one most responsive to change.
—Charles Darwin

chapter 3

Welcome to Law School

So Much to Learn
Before Classes Even Begin

Before moving inside those ivy-covered (or not) walls of your new world, we come to the most significant message of your law school endeavor. It is with the following information that I lead you forward to pursue your dreams. If you feel a natural affinity towards living by the standards set forth in the following paragraphs, then, perhaps you have found your true calling. If not, then you still have time to turn back.

Honor Thy Self

There is an honor code in law school. It might not be posted, but it does exist. It is crucial to the environment, as well as the profession. This often unspoken code needs to be discussed early, as it is extremely important that you understand its significance.

The honor code is not a list of rules posted on the wall for you to follow as you did in grade school. Of course, there will be written rules that must be abided by as in all educational institutions. However, the code of honor in law school is something that you are either born with or have come to understand through life experience. It cannot be clearly defined. You are just somehow able to recognize it and you will hopefully feel comfortable about following it.

Some educational institutions post signs regarding the dangers of leaving possessions unattended in the library or in other areas of their school. They utilize proctors to walk the aisles during exams to ensure that nobody has the opportunity to cheat. There are strict policies about make-up exams differing from the originals to ensure that nobody is given the test questions ahead of time. Other rules are in place to enforce an honest environment. However, there are some schools that do not find it necessary to employ those means to keep their students on the straight and narrow.

EXHIBIT

A close friend attended a well-known southern law school. He was from New York, had gone to college in New York, and was enrolled at a law school where the honor code was self-enforcing. At first, he was thrilled at the thought of being so free to do as he pleased. But it was not long before he fell into step with the code. What had happened, he explained, was an inner feeling of duty—a duty to live up to the respect and trust that had been bestowed upon him for no other reason than an expectation of honesty. It was not about signs or proctors. In the end, he had to be true to himself.

He said that the honor code he learned to live by reached out into his daily life. He was not a dishonest person, but his outlook on life changed when he learned that he had not been living in total honesty. For example, one day, he noticed a highlighter sitting on a library table. Prior to starting law school, he may have thought that if someone left it behind for a long enough period of time, it was up for grabs. But now, he saw things from a different vantage point. Although he did use the pen occasionally when he had forgotten his own, he never removed it from that table—and nobody else did either—for an entire semester.

To understand the difference between an environment in which constant surveillance exists and one where there is a self-enforcing code of honor, you must be able to recognize that rules are made by individuals who are reacting to their own surroundings and the value system that they themselves possess. You have to assume that these rules came into existence only *after* a substantial amount of dishonesty occurred to warrant their creation. You always want to believe that the trust that originated there was somehow broken and that no choice was left but to set up a code of enforcement.

No matter where you attend law school, the honor code that you will be expected to follow is not about written rules or punishments. It is not about being monitored to ensure compliance. It is about the way in which you live your life and the respect that you give to yourself and others. It is the way that you will spend your three years at law school and the manner in which you will hopefully run your practice. You are duty-bound, not because there are consequences if you do not comply, but because you will ultimately sleep better if you do.

Live up to your own self-imposed, high standards regardless of the law of the land. You will reap many rewards. While others are being taught to hide law books from the competition or keep helpful materials to themselves so as not to assist anyone else in getting better grades, you can be the model, the example for all to follow. Show your generosity by sharing your notes, your knowledge, and your friendship with others. Do not hesitate to spend a moment clearing up a confusing point for a classmate who seems a bit lost. Your desired profession warrants that you are honest and that you show compassion, understanding, and assistance to those who come to you for guidance and representation. Let those character traits begin in law school and extend to all who know you, as well as all who seek your direction. They will carry you a long way in the legal world and in life.

Re-Orientation

Once you enter the law school building, you will experience emotions previously unknown to you. At times, you will doubt your own sanity, your intellect, and your motives for being there. You will have penetrated an environment where the way of life is not within your present realm of comprehension. You will be required to master a foreign language. You will suffer from fatigue, inadequate nutrition, and acute anxiety.

However, law school does not have to be totally disagreeable. For the most part, it is just another place where you receive an education. How you adjust to the rigorous schedule is very much up to you. Stressing out does not make you perform better, so why bother? Taking things slowly and focusing on important details is key. There are shortcuts to be found. Some are beneficial, while others will only assist you in being shortchanged. So beware and be alert to what is actually being asked of you. The more you pay attention and follow directions, the easier your stay will be.

Law school will commence when you acquire your first-year schedule and your invitation to orientation. When you are invited to attend orientation, go! It will be your first take on what to expect over the next three years. Upon arrival, talk to those around you. Since you already have your schedule, try to find students who will be in your classes. They may become some of your closest friends during the months to follow. You will need a support system where you will look for someone to anchor you during the upcoming and somewhat turbulent times. Take advantage of orientation to make those contacts. It is a fairly informal environment and everyone is searching for a friendly face to soften the somewhat rigid introduction that you all will receive.

Prepare to hear welcome speeches from various distinguished members of the faculty. They will most likely not sugarcoat the hardships of law school life. You will probably be told to look to your right and look to your left because one of you will not make it to graduation. You will give great thought to this. *One of us will be gone? One out of every three of us will not be able to handle this?* Hearing that is a very unsettling prelude to an otherwise stress-filled day. You will also be told that those of you who *do* survive will be expected to excel. You are somewhat secure in thinking that you, in fact, *will* excel. After all, you did very well as an undergrad. But, as you gaze around, you begin to feel a bit uneasy. You are looking into the faces of all of those other over-achievers who have been accepted into the same school as you. As the faculty members continue speaking, you feel a sense of disorder lingering in the air. People are looking around, taking an inventory of those sitting near them. Even *you* are becoming unnerved. *How can we all excel?* you wonder.

As the minutes pass, you begin to assume that it is all or nothing—succeed or fail with no room in between for mediocre performance. That is how your mind was trained to think *pre*-law school. However, during the next three years, you will learn to see the gray area, the place that holds a truth that you have yet to experience. Before law school, there existed merely black and white, right or wrong. Bad people lost. Good people won. Here, there is an endless, ashen plane where questions are analyzed and dissected and answers are challenged, contradicted, disputed, and debated. Time after time, you will be left wondering, always searching for an answer; and the one thing that you will come to be very sure of is that, where the law is concerned, you can never be sure of anything.

Take a deep breath and relax. Now you know why attending orientation is essential. But remember to take what you hear with a grain of salt and keep your fears to a minimum. Attempt to use orientation day to *network* with others to create the early support system that you will so desperately need in the months to follow. More importantly, allow yourself the luxury of keeping an open mind at all times until you are able to clearly envision those gray areas in life and in the law that you have yet to even imagine.

Avoiding First-Day Fumbles

You arrive on campus for your first day of law school and frantically run through the building looking for your torts class. The hallways are crowded with students rushing around trying to find their way, but the rooms are not in any particular order. You scan number after number on the classroom doors until you finally come across room 202. When you peek inside, you see that everyone is already seated and the professor is lecturing. You're not sure what to do, but you don't want to miss the first class. So, breathing heavily, you bolt through the door.

You blurt out that you could not find the room because it's your first day. Then, you collapse into the nearest empty seat. You fumble through your belongings trying to find a pen and some paper. Suddenly, you notice the silence. The professor has not continued with his lecture and everyone is staring at you. You feel uneasy. You begin to sweat. It's too quiet. It feels a lot like one of those *late for school on the day of final exams and I don't know a thing* nightmares that everyone has. You wonder why he doesn't say something . You are almost afraid to make eye contact with him. Just then, an earthshattering voice breaks the silence.

Excuse me, Mister…what is your name, sir? the professor queries. You stutter, trying to remember your own name. *I - I'm Mister Smith, Jack Smith, Sir. Well, Mr. Jack Smith, Sir, this is not college, nor, is it high school. You are late! You are disruptive and you will not be permitted to stumble into the courtroom that way. So do not presume to think that you can enter my classroom like that! Do you understand, Mister Jack Smith, Sir?* While nodding your head in the affirmative, you slink down into your seat, certain that you will never recover from this humiliation. Your thoughts are racing, *It's the first day and I've blown it already. He's going to fail me for sure!*

Take heart—you *will* recover. But more importantly, you do not have to go through that harrowing nightmare in the first place. The following suggestions are important to your survival in law school, especially for avoiding the previous scenario. Familiarity with your environment is key to feeling less disoriented.

Before Classes Begin

Visit your law school before classes begin. Take the time to familiarize yourself with your new surroundings. You will receive your class schedule prior to the commencement of classes. Bring it with you to make sure that you will know where you are going on your first day. There is nothing worse than walking into a law school class late.

The Law Library

This is where you will spend much of your first semester while being introduced to the task of legal research. As you will soon learn, legal research is the cornerstone of your legal education.

As you enter the law library, you may detect the sudden drop in temperature. You might want to have a sweater or jacket with you. It is noticeably cold. In the weeks to follow, you will soon come to realize that there is a strategy behind this morgue-like frigidity. It is what you will shortly learn to be an admission by law school personnel that they must do something, *anything*, to keep your head from crashing into your law books while you are doing your work. In other words, they are acknowledging that your material is, for the most part, boring, colorless, mundane, and tedious. But, take heart—cold air *is* healthy!

There will be a section in your library where the carrels are located. Carrels are simply desks and they are sometimes assigned to specific students. In many schools, this is the one place where a student can escape to feel safe from the hectic surroundings. In a small way, it will be your home away from home. Depending on your school, carrels can be adorned with pictures of the student's friends and family and mementos that remind him or her that there *is* life outside of law school.

The Assignment Board

In most schools, assignments and notices are posted prior to the commencement of classes and at regular intervals throughout the semester. You are expected to be well prepared for class *on your first day* of school. Thus, be sure to find the assignment board early on. Check it regularly, especially after each and every class, for new assignments and information regarding class cancellations, make-up classes, room changes, and various other items pertinent to being fully informed. There is no excuse for not knowing what is expected of you if it is posted on that board.

You may also receive a new email account through the school's system. Some professors will send notices by email. Be sure to check it regularly.

The Bookstore

Before the first day, purchase your books, study aids, and necessary reference guides. In law school you will be expected to have everything you need on the first day.

CASEBOOKS

Your text books are actually considered *casebooks* in law school.

Your bookstore should be able to correlate your schedule with the books that you need. Be prepared to spend a few hundred dollars on your books and supplies.

Unless they are highlighted and marked-up beyond comprehension, buy used books. They are substantially cheaper than new ones and if you can find ones that are not too bad, simply buy magic markers that are different colors than the ones already there to enable you to differentiate between what *you* think is important and what the last person who had the book wanted to remember.

STUDY AIDS

Purchase the *study aids* that correspond with your casebooks. The bookstore personnel will be able to guide you towards the appropriate aids. These are books that are often written specifically with your casebooks in mind. Some serve the purpose of *briefing* cases (to be discussed later) for you and explaining them. Others give a general outline of the course. Once you have become familiar with these aids, you will view them as lifesavers in the pool of muck and mire.

BLACK'S LAW DICTIONARY

Purchase *Black's Law Dictionary*. This is your translation guide for the unfamiliar lingo that you will be reading and hearing. It is doubtful that there is a lawyer who does not have one of these in either the large, hardcover version or the small, paperback style.

Legal jargon, otherwise known as *legalese*, is a foreign language and you will need your *translation guide* at all times during your first year (if not thereafter). Do not assume that a familiar word is really what it seems to be.

> **Example:** If you hear that someone will *make an appearance*, you may think it means that they are going to just show up somewhere. However, in legal terms, it means that an attorney will be in court giving notice that he or she is representing his or her client.

> **Example:** The word *reservation* may bring thoughts of a dinner date or land belonging to Native Americans. In legal jargon, it is a provision in a deed reserving to the grantor some right pertaining to a piece of property.

Use your law dictionary often, especially during reading assignments, to stay on top of the new language that you will be required to understand.

BLUEBOOK

Purchase the *Bluebook*. This is the *Uniform System of Citation*. Citation is the roadmap to locating written pieces, such as a cases, statutes, periodicals, and many other publications. The book is especially important for learning how to cite case law. Most lawyers, if not all, are familiar with this small, generally mandatory, book.

SUPPLIES

Purchase highlighting pens. You should buy a few different colors in order to create a system for *briefing* as you read through your assignments.

Purchase notebooks. Each person has preferences regarding what type of notebooks to use. Loose leafs are practical because, if a student misses a class, notes are easily removed to copy and reinsert back into the proper place.

> **NOTE:** You will take several pages of notes per class. Do not assume that you can miss a day's notes and it will not matter. You cannot catch up by simply reading your assignments. Get the notes and study them!

Technological advances have allowed many law schools to provide connections for students to hook their laptops up to for note-taking during classes. There are distinct advantages to using the laptop over a notebook. Some of the advantages include the following.

- You will not have to write at a furiously fast pace, making it necessary for you to stop and shake out your hand at regular intervals.
- You will not run out of ink in the middle of serious note taking.
- You will not have to worry about being unable to read your own messy handwriting several hours (or days later) while reviewing your hastily written notes.
- More importantly, you will not have to rewrite your notes to prepare your class outlines (to be discussed later). You can simply delete the unimportant dribble and use the outlining features provided in your laptop.

Now that you know your way around campus and have all of your school supplies, it's time for classes to begin.

First Year Quarantine

In the majority of law schools, first-year students are assigned to their *sections*, as well as their *classes*. Sections are made up of groups of students who stay together in the same classes throughout the first year. In my school, there were three first-year sections, A, B, and C. Each section consisted of approximately one hundred students.

There is definitely something to be said for this system. The stress of first-year law can be overwhelming; seeing the same familiar faces each and every day can provide a sense of continuity and reassurance. You have the advantage of becoming close to your classmates. During an incredibly anxiety-ridden year when you feel extremely isolated from all that you were connected to pre-law, it is especially comforting to know that there is at least one constant in the whirlwind of law school.

Your first year schedule will consist of at least five to six year-long courses, including a legal research and writing class, all of which will be extremely demanding. If you miss a class, you miss an important chunk of material that is difficult to make up by merely getting someone else's notes. Although it is not out of the question to use other students' notes to keep up when it comes to some classes, especially upper level courses, the first year is also a time when attendance is carefully monitored. Even if it isn't, you should attend because keeping up with class lectures and assignments is more important for you than for your professor.

It is crucial that you stay on top of your workload. It is also essential that you become fully accustomed with what your professor expects from you regarding class participation, exams, and papers. Understanding their requirements is the only way to achieve success, and to do this, you must be familiar with and able to adjust to their particular mode of instruction.

Besides being assigned to your section, you will also be assigned your first-year class schedule. This is nonnegotiable. You must stay with your section in each and every class.

First-year classes are meant to introduce you to all of the key concepts required to understand the legal system. The following is a brief description of what will generally be included in your first-year courses.

CIVIL PROCEDURE

Civil Procedure describes how a civil lawsuit is brought and the *procedural path* that it takes to get through the court system. You will learn about such topics as who has *standing* (the right to initiate a lawsuit); which court has *jurisdiction* (the authority to adjudicate a particular case); what types of jurisdiction exist; the *statute of limitations* (at what point the time runs out to commence an action); and many other issues involving how to function in the legal system.

TORT LAW

Tort Law involves *civil liability* for acts committed by persons or government entities. In other words, who will be held responsible for a slip and fall; a car accident; a foreign object in food; a doctor's or lawyer's malpractice; false imprisonment; and many more claims that do not fall within the criminal category. *Duty*, *breach* of that duty, *harm*, *remedies*, and *defenses* are also discussed, as well as the difference between an *intentional act* and a *negligent one*.

CONTRACT LAW

Contract Law analyzes what it takes to create a binding agreement, to breach it, and what remedies are available to satisfy the agreement. Discussed are the concepts of *offer*, *acceptance*, and *consideration*, and how they create a *binding contract*. To put it simply, a contract is created when one person makes a promise to do something in exchange for someone else's promise to do something else. Of course, this is a primitive explanation, but it gives you an idea of what a contract is.

CONSTITUTIONAL LAW

Constitutional Law may be one of the most important classes during your law school tenure. In some schools, this is a first-year course. In others, it is taken later on. Here you will learn that the United States Constitution serves as the supreme law of the land. It is where all of our rights and privileges as United States citizens are found. It is the document by which we challenge our government when it appears that those rights and privileges are being abridged. It is then up to the Supreme Court to interpret the Constitution in a way that allows us to fully realize and understand our rights. Since the document is subject to interpretation, there is no guarantee of a win in the Supreme Court. However, by researching prior Supreme Court decisions (*precedents*), we become better able to argue our cases in a reasonably capable manner and to predict the likelihood of success in front of the Court.

This course also teaches the basics of how the powers of the federal and state governments are kept separate, how the legislative, judicial and executive branches function under those powers, and why it is necessary that there are separate and distinct branches of government. Thus, if you find yourself being discriminated against due to race, religion, gender, handicap, or any one of a number of other constitutionally protected things, or if you are told that you are forbidden from speaking your mind, writing about a certain subject, participating in a specific type of event, or denied your day in court, it is the Constitution to which you will look for protection.

CRIMINAL LAW

In a few short words, a *Criminal Law* course teaches you how to determine what type of behavior is necessary for an act to be considered a crime; the procedural steps to take regarding what type of punishments may be administered; and what constitutional protections are afforded to protect the defendant. You will learn about the difference between committing a crime with intent or preparation and committing a crime out of emotional upset. You will also learn how a person may be guilty of committing a crime just for going along for the ride or discussing the crime with the perpetrator before it happens and not doing something to prevent it from taking place.

PROPERTY LAW

Property Law tends to be somewhat more complicated in comparison to the others. Generally, the student learns about the development of property law dating back to the feudal period of England and spanning to the present day (which is good because you will finally begin to more easily understand the language). Covered are *landlord/tenant disputes*, *personal property issues*, and *estate interests*.

> **NOTE:** Many students walk into this course thinking that it is all about real estate. But the famous *Pierson v. Post* case demonstrates otherwise. It involves chasing and catching a fox, and at what point, if ever, possession of the fox is truly achieved. There are law schools where nearly an entire semester will be spent on this case alone.

LEGAL RESEARCH AND WRITING

Legal Research and Writing is probably the most indispensable class in law school. These are the essential ingredients for getting through law school and successfully practicing law. Legal writing is the lawyer's artillery. It is through the art of communication that the lawyer makes his or her point. A well-written motion, a thought-provoking *brief*, a craftily-drafted *contract*, or a simple *letter of intent* can all serve as devices that make the difference between winning or losing a case and closing or killing a deal. Your pen is your sword and the more capable you are at putting pen to paper, the more successful you will be in your practice of law.

In your legal writing course, you will be guided through the steps of *brief* and *memoranda* writing, advised regarding which books and resources are the most useful for research on specific topics, taught methods to analyze those issues, and finally, you will learn how to properly weave it all together to make your point. Most legal research and writing classes culminate with the writing of a *brief*, and depending upon the school, a *moot court argument*.

During first-year law, you may find it somewhat unsettling if you are consistently criticized for your writing skills, or lack thereof, especially if you were a highly successful English student in college. But it is important to remember that there is a huge difference between creative college composition and fact-based law school writing.

At the beginning of the course, you will attempt to draft elaborate papers similar to those you wrote in college English. You will take the information given to you and weave tales around it, embellishing and crafting details to make them more interesting. You will proudly turn it in and wait for your professor's critique, feeling relieved at how easily you completed your assignment. However, you and your paper will be often be chewed up and spit out if there is even a hint of creativity in it.

Facts, facts, and more facts! That is what legal writing is all about. Your professors do not want to hear that the *sharp, red-stained knife that was used to kill the tiny waif of a child was still dripping with her poor, little body's red blood.* More to the point would be that the *murder weapon tested positive for the victim's blood.* (Creative writing does not belong in the factual world of law.)

Discover Your Own Secrets for Success

Once you understand that you really *do* belong in law school, if not because you have figured out how to overcome some of the many obstacles, but because you realize that you are no more confused than the students sitting to your left and right, you will spend some serious time trying to determine exactly what steps you need to take in order to succeed in this environment. You will come to understand that part of the secret of law school success is simply having the ability to complete a task in as few steps as possible.

EXHIBIT

A third-year law student told me that one particular thing that enabled her to survive first-year law was to hook up with law fellows, upper class students who had performed very well in their first year.

Law fellows will assist you in wading through the unimportant garble and focusing on the necessary elements of what the professor is trying to instill in you. If your school does not have law fellows, then find an upper class person and pick his or her brain. The law fellow or upper class student should ideally be someone who has taken the same courses as you with the same professors.

Ask your law fellow the following questions.

- What types of study aides are the most helpful?
- Are there any good student-made class outlines circulating?
- Who are the best professors and why?
- Which bar review courses are the best?

Study Aids

There are many study aids that some students find extremely helpful. Some of the more popular ones are discussed below.

COMMERCIAL OUTLINES

Commercial outlines provide detailed outlines of each course. They are extremely helpful for purposes of pulling a course together. However, they are fairly general and may not include certain points that your professor considers significant.

The most popular brands of outlines include:
- *Emanuel's*;
- *Gilbert's*;
- *Legalines*; and,
- *Sum and Substance*.

CASE NOTE'S

Case Note's are legal briefs that may correspond with your particular casebooks. They relieve you of the burden of reading and briefing cases. However, these are not to be used as a substitute for reading your assignments and understanding how to brief the cases yourself.

> **NOTE:** Briefing a case properly (to be discussed later) is an art form, and most of the questions that you will be asked in class are for the sole purpose of helping you to read, brief, and understand case law, not just for purposes of school, but for your practice of law.

IN A NUTSHELL

In a Nutshell are paperback reference books that provide thorough summaries of specific areas of law. For example, most law school book stores carry *Torts, In a Nutshell* or *Criminal Law, In a Nutshell*.

HORNBOOKS AND TREATISES

Hornbooks and treatises are generally written by law professors and more closely resemble your college texts than law school books. They are assembled by subject matter and written in lay language that is much more easily understood than the case law that you will be struggling to decipher.

AUDIO AND VIDEO TAPES

These aids are usually not as valuable a tool as the books described earlier. However, they do provide a convenient mechanism for reviewing material simply because you can close your eyes and listen. They can also travel with you when you are on the go, giving you additional study time. They are beneficial devices for getting a general picture of the key concepts of a subject rather than an indepth description of each course.

FLASH CARDS

Flash cards should bring back fond memories of childhood. They are a bit more complicated then the ones used in elementary school, but, the general idea is the same—questions or concepts on one side, answers on the other.

STUDY GROUPS

There is something to be said for bouncing ideas off of other people. *Study groups* are a great way to review the course work with fellow students and gain valuable feedback about your ideas, as well as your uncertainties. When groups of compatible students meet regularly, it reinforces the learning process and serves as a beneficial support system in a very stressful environment.

However, beware of what one student referred to as *hangers-on.* These are students who do not work as hard as you do. They may be falling behind and looking to latch onto those students who are staying on top of their work. In that case, being in a study group with hangers on will not be productive because there will be no give and take, no one to bounce ideas off of or to get feedback from. It may as well be a tutoring session. Find other students who are in the same place academically as you.

STUDENT-MADE OUTLINES

As will be expanded upon later, an *outline* is an abbreviated rendering of your class notes. The best outlines are the ones prepared by the students, themselves. They are beneficial for two important reasons.

First, the student who prepares it has reviewed the material and broken it down into a capsulized version of an entire semester's work. Key points are emphasized, and often flow charts are prepared to enable the student to easily follow a course from beginning to end. This is hard work and it takes time. It is a wonderful source of review for the person who creates it.

Second, for the student who receives someone else's skillfully crafted outline, it can be an invaluable way to follow a course from its inception while allowing the students to know and understand ahead of time what is expected of them. It will also assist the student who is not a strong note-taker to pull the course together at the end of the semester for the purpose of studying for exams. Generally, it is best to get the outline from someone who has taken the same course as you with the same professor. Most often, professors follow the same curriculum from one year to the next and a good outline can generally pass through a number of hands before it becomes obsolete—if ever.

Professors

Asking who the best professors are and why is a question ideally asked while preparing to register for second- and third-year courses when you will finally have the opportunity to create your own schedule. Each professor has his or her own unique method for teaching. Sometimes, it is obvious that certain professors are not for you (or for anyone, for that matter). Receiving feedback from other students can assist you in gaining insight into what the professor's teaching method is like, what he or she expects from students, and how rigid or flexible he or she is about such things as class participation and attendance.

EXHIBIT

An attorney who had been very careful to register for classes one semester with only certain professors said that she had taken the advice of a fellow student who had gotten "A's." Unfortunately, she did not ask anything about the professors' teaching styles, the type of classroom participation required, the assignments given, or the methods for grading. She was quite surprised to find herself in a very uncomfortable situation. She did fine, but, not without a struggle.

Remember to ask about those important details because you must feel that the situation is one that you can adapt to comfortably. Of course, due to scheduling conflicts and class size limits, you will not always be able to choose your favorite professors. But do not despair. You will not choose your first-year professors and you *will* survive their teaching methods.

Bar Review Courses

It is only first year and you may be wondering why you should be thinking about the bar exam so soon. The exam is, without a doubt, the most important one you will ever take. It means the difference between being able to practice law or not. Since there are advantages (to be discussed later) to signing up early for a course, it is beneficial to find out as soon as possible which one will work for you. The organizations that offer bar review courses for the state where your law school is located often have sales representatives who visit the school and actively promote their particular program. While various companies have different programs, BarBri dominates the market and provides review courses for every state. Visit its website at **www.barbri.org** to get information about your state.

Socrates Who?

In law school, you will generally not experience the style of teaching that you came across in college. Now you will most likely encounter what is known as the *Socratic method* of teaching. Briefly, this means that the professor will ask countless questions without ever giving answers. This approach is meant to stimulate your mind and allow you to fully dissect a problem prior to coming to a conclusion, rather than just giving a text book answer and moving on.

The purpose behind this dueling of words is to help you recognize right up front that there are no real answers, no absolutes to depend upon. The law is as unpredictable as the weather. That is why each case is *adjudicated* separately. No two cases hold identical facts. You must understand early in your law career that thinking independently, analytically, and coherently is essential to formulating a winning strategy.

So as you sit in class, you will often cower in your seat waiting for your turn to not have an answer. And, as the perspiration drips down the back of your neck, you will experience that familiar feeling that you had in junior high when you kept your eye on the clock while praying for the bell to ring, so you could run out of the room before being called upon. You *will* be called upon. And, when your turn comes, you may very well find yourself at the receiving end of a thirty minute grilling—something akin to cross-examination—which, if you are lucky, you will be able to respond to with a slight measure of intelligence.

INTO THE FIRE

The *Socratic method* is only one of several styles of instruction. While it is common in law school classes, every professor has his or her own way of doing things. This includes how students are called upon to participate in the class lecture.

EXHIBIT

An attorney said that the law school he attended had several student-named approaches for being grilled in class. One such approach was the *Machine-Gun* method where the professor would shoot question after question, spinning around and pointing at a different shell-shocked student each time. He would quickly thrust his arm forward with a finger extended and ask, "What is the case name?" He would swing around and demand, "What is the holding?" Then, pivoting to the left, "What court was the case brought in?" Charging to the right, "What was the dissenting opinion?"

Other professors choose the more predictable *alphabet* approach where students are called on in alphabetical order. This method allows students to be fairly secure in knowing when they will be called upon, thereby enabling them the most latitude for preparation.

Another line of questioning is the *random* approach where there is no known method for the selection of who will be called upon. This method has the effect of keeping all students on their toes at all times.

Then there is the *punishment* method, where a professor asks a certain number of questions and when he was sufficiently satisfied that no answer would rise to his or her level of satisfaction, the professor throws the entire class out of the room.

Of course, there will be those professors (though few and far between) who will ask a question and wait for someone to actually raise their hand. If none goes up, a name will inevitably be chosen at random. If you are not prepared and you go through the standard grilling and humiliation sessions enough times, you will hopefully get with the program and do your best to be ready for the next wave of cross-examination. Otherwise, it will not be long before you begin to question whose mistake it was that allowed you to be accepted into law school in the first place. But remember, while having to answer questions in class may seem stressful, you are feeling no different than everyone else.

chapter 4

Non Illegitimi Carborundum

(Don't Let the Bastards Grind You Down)

Now that you have been shown some of the ins and outs of first-year law, you are going to be given a peek behind the scenes to see what they don't tell you at orientation.

Handling It All

It is eleven o'clock at night and you have just finished reading a sixty-five page assignment for your contracts class. You have a first-draft due tomorrow on your legal writing paper, it is your turn to be called on in civil procedure, and you have not even had a chance to read the lengthy assignment or brief the cases for that class.

So you:
1. Cry uncontrollably and throw your books out the window.
2. Pack your belongings and run home to mommy and daddy.
3. Tell your professors that your dog ate your work.
4. Make a pot of coffee and stay up all night getting as much work done as possible.

If you chose anything besides #4, you are not on the right track for surviving law school. There are various ways to deal with the pressure, but panicking is not one of them. However, going with the flow and doing your work instead of allowing it to overwhelm you will help you to overcome the stress and keep a clear head and focused mind. Swimming against the tide only wears you out.

Remember, everyone feels the pressure and only those who stay calm and level-headed survive the experience.

Areas exist for relieving a bit of the stress of law school. There are counselors, study guides, pamphlets, books, seminars, workshops, and various other means for learning how to reduce some of the tension of exams, spontaneous questioning by professors, moot court arguments, job interviews, etc. Unfortunately, by the time most students search for relief, their blood pressure is off the charts and they are in such a state that they have already fallen behind substantially. It then becomes a struggle to reach the point where they can regain some composure.

The most advantageous time to work on your state of mind is *before* you enter the arena. A boxer never walks into the ring cold. He or she prepares tirelessly before meeting the challenge and so should you. Of course, there will be those times when your stress level is going to escalate, no matter how well-prepared you are, like the morning of an exam or when you know that tomorrow is your turn in the hot seat in class. Realizing ahead of time what to expect will always minimize the anticipatory panic attack.

Even when you think you have gotten a bit more accustomed to the law school environment, you may soon realize that you are becoming more, not less nervous as time passes. You will have attended orientation where you have been told that one out of every three of you will be gone by graduation. You will have struggled through confusing assignments. You will have agonized through disconcerting lectures. You will become somewhat disillusioned because the things that you understood so clearly through college are no longer relevant in this environment.

Law school is a lot of hard work. You will be awake until all hours of the night trying to keep up and absorb what you read. You will often wonder what the heck you are reading, because you have no idea yet what a tort is, or what the rule against perpetuities is, and you will certainly have no understanding of the endless cases that you are expected to know well enough to be able to answer a barrage of questions about in class. As you complete each assign-ment, you will become more and more confused. You will stare blankly at information that you have read, re-read, re-re-read, and re-re-re-read.

The secret here is to recognize when it is time to close your books and go to sleep, because this is not a situation where you are merely tired and words are not making sense anymore. Many of the words will not make sense when you are wide awake. So, why strug-gle in the middle of the night to grasp something that is already beyond your comprehension? Tomorrow is another day and hope-fully, you will hear explanations in class for what you do not under-stand about the material. If not, ask a law fellow or walk into your professor's office and discuss the matter. If all else fails, it is time to realize that you are probably not the only one who is lost. So, let it go and move on to the next reading. The key to remember is that all of the readings are meant to introduce you to caselaw and how it comes about and evolves. The basics of a subject are woven into all of that, and once you know the basics, even if a case seems over your head, you will still be able to survive the course. So do not panic.

Isolation, Intimidation, and Humiliation

A difficult part of law school is the isolation that many students experience. You are woven into an environment where you will spend each day, day after day, being indoctrinated with new ideas. At the same time, you will be surrounded by the same forlorn faces over and over. You are in a place where stress and anxiety thrive at their highest levels. You are far away from home, even if only emo-tionally, for what seems like an eternity, and you are much too busy for anything or anyone in the outside world. You feel very much alone, especially during the first few months when you are still new to this somewhat sterile, unappealing landscape.

EXHIBIT

One student referred to this as the "P.O.W. Effect." He said he had been totally wrapped up in his law studies, staying up around the clock, reading assignments and briefing cases, spending hours researching in the library, working with study groups, and writing papers. After several weeks, he allowed himself a brief respite and left the school to meet his friend in town for dinner. As he walked down the street, he passed a couple holding hands and eyed some guys riding bikes. A movie was letting out and people were chatting excitedly about the plot. *What's going on?* he thought. Stopping for a moment, he stared at his surroundings. He noticed the smiles on people's faces, heard laughter in the air, and smelled the sweet aroma of flowers coming from a nearby display. *Man*, he thought, *I feel like a prisoner of war who has finally escaped. I've been so inundated with school work that I had forgotten that life outside of law school had not come to a complete halt.*

This is a typical reaction to first-year law school. To succeed, you must devote your entire energies to the tasks assigned. You study, you read, you brief, you sit in class, work in the library, grab a quick bite to eat in the school lounge where you sit and study and read and brief. Then, you go back to your room and study some more until you awaken in the morning with your face in your book, and you have to get up and do it all over again.

It is common to feel completely enveloped by the law school experience and to succumb to the pressure by overworking. Unfortunately, this only drives you deeper into the law school dungeon and you become more likely to fall prey to the possibility of giving up or failing. You must learn to pace yourself. Make time to close your books and regroup. Try to maintain even the smallest sense of a social life. The best you will do for companionship is to share those rigorous moments with others who are also being indoctrinated into this often static, unyielding environment. It is not easy at first, but before long, if you are well-prepared, you do become accustomed to the routine as well as the isolation.

Beer Here

Some schools attempt to help relieve the pressure by organizing on-campus get-togethers. This is a good way to meet students who are not in your section and to have some down time without straying too far from your books.

EXHIBIT

An attorney remembered fondly his school's regular Friday night keg parties. He said that it was a great way to escape the daily grind and forget about the demands of law school.

The competitive environment of law school requires a great deal of commitment and discipline. It is only normal that students look for an *out* from their demanding surroundings. However, by holding weekly keg parties, some schools are providing an alcohol-induced escape from a harsh reality of its own making. This may seem like a drastic statement, but, alcohol and drug abuse are growing problems in the legal profession.

Recognizing the potential for abuse may be all you need to do to avoid future problems. There is nothing wrong with going out and having a few beers with friends once in awhile. Everyone needs to kick back and let their hair down. It is important to rejuvenate yourself while at law school, if not at an occasional keg party, then, at a movie, a baseball game, or any other outside activity that helps you to keep some semblance of a normal life. But you must keep things in the proper perspective and try to balance yourself so that you learn how to handle the pressure without having to resort to over-indulging in substances that anesthetize you.

EXHIBIT

The same attorney who went to the keg parties said that very early on in his law career, a wise mentor gave him the following advice: "Every attorney should become an expert in three hobbies that have nothing at all to do with law." So he chose the Civil War, baseball, and marathon running. He said it was probably the best advice that he has been given, because rather than reliving the Friday night binging as many of his colleagues do, he has always had a healthy outlet for his stress.

Work hard, but make sure life does not pass you by. As hard as it may be, and it is difficult at times, close your books, take a walk outside and smell the flowers. Refresh yourself and go back to your schoolwork with a clear head. Do not let the stress corner you. And whatever you do, do not give up!

Method to the Madness

Feeling intimidated and humiliated in front of your peers is difficult to tolerate. Nobody wants to be in a situation where you are struggling to do your best, but no matter how hard you try, you just cannot seem to get it right in your professor's eyes. However, as mentioned earlier, it is a fact of law school life that at one time or another, you will be sitting in the hot seat. You will be put on the spot to answer questions that you cannot answer. You will be reprimanded for not knowing and accused of not being prepared for class. Chances are, you really were prepared. You were probably up all night doing your work. Yet, you have no way of proving it. You know that if you insist that you did your reading, you will look even more foolish, because you were unable to answer your professor's questions. You will feel helpless—like crawling under your desk and waiting for the storm to blow over. Your mind will race with thoughts about this unimaginable cruelty. You will often wonder, *How can he justify making me feel so small in front of everyone?*

EXHIBIT

An attorney described one of her professors as loud and considerably intimidating. She said that while questioning a student who was apparently unprepared, he repeatedly reprimanded him, finally telling him that he did not belong in the class or law school and insisted that he pack up his books and get out. She said that it was hard to tolerate the situation as they all sat there shaking in their seats, feeling completely empathetic towards their fellow classmate. The biggest surprise came, she said, when the student finally got up and headed for the door. He was once again strongly reprimanded. This time, it was for not fighting back by arguing with the professor about why he belonged there!

The truth is, there *is* a method to all of this madness. There are valid reasons for this treatment. Most often, your professor is not the cruelest person on Earth. He or she is generally just trying to prepare you for the real world—yes, the *REAL* world. This is *only* school. No matter how hard you try to convince yourself that this is the most important place in the world to be, it is not! This is the test, the training program. This is where you go to prepare for the real thing. Do not get caught up in taking it so seriously that your world begins and ends with how well your day goes. In short, do not let this place break you.

Your professor will most likely know that you did do the reading, because even if you are not giving the answers that are being demanded of you, you *are* giving answers. This indicates that you did read your assignment, even if you did not understand or remember it. So do not sweat it if you are not on the same wavelength as your professor for the moment. You are merely the one who is on the rack today. Tomorrow, it will be someone else. Every day for the rest of the semester, somebody will feel tormented. Everyone survives if they understand how the system works and why it needs to work that way.

Generally, what you consider to be harsh treatment in law school is one way that you will become familiar with what life as an attorney can be like, especially, but not only, if you become a litigator. Courtroom practice is a difficult challenge and being thick-skinned and capable of thinking on your feet are essential characteristics. You will be facing adversaries who will be trying their best to trip you up to win an argument. You will be confronted by judges (some of whom have been on the bench for the better part of half a century) who will grill you and test you in their own way. They will not think twice about admonishing you if you are unprepared or incapable of arguing your case properly. Judges are famous for challenging attorneys and demanding case law cites to back up a position.

The point is that some of those so-called horrible teaching methods that you will encounter in law school are for the sole purpose of preparing you for the courtroom. If you can retain your composure, you will find the words to move on, even if they are not exactly what the judge wants. Keeping your cool and being able to think on your feet helps you to survive in the world of law.

Unfortunately, in school, there will also be those situations where you will be confronted by a professor whose time has come to leave the classroom, but who has not yet recognized the need to be away from the lectern. They are not the rule, but they do exist and they can be quite crass. There may not always be a good reason for your humiliating moments, but just the same, you will not be alone in your torment in the classroom. Someday, you may also be faced with a judge whose gavel should have long since been put to rest. You have to learn to roll with the punches and survive the moment either way.

One more point about why you may have difficult moments during your law school education is that your kindergarten teacher most likely had more training to become an educator than your law professors. Attorneys walk into a classroom the same way they would enter the courtroom, aggressively and with a prepared curriculum that they rarely stray from. More often than not, you are going to get a real dose of courtroom-type tactics rather than a smooth transition into new subject areas and the delivery of material in a palatable way. This is a training ground for the behavior that comes with the territory of being an attorney, and you are experiencing it every day in school. It is just part of the initiation into the legal world. Each time you survive another day of this initiation faze, there is a great sense of relief. It is one more indication to you that law school is doable. You need this reassurance, and you should allow yourself to recognize that what used to seem like the smallest accomplishment in college is now a huge hurdle that you have cleared.

As you move forward, the important thing to remember is that this is only school. Do not let it define who you are, because with each new day, you become more and more capable of succeeding in this environment. Make time to experience life in the outside world. The most successful law school students are those who can stay focused, but who do not take themselves or anyone else so seriously that they forget about being able to close their books and relax. Do not do more work than is required. Find the shortcuts that are best suited for you and will not shortchange your legal education. Keep telling yourself that there is a method to the madness that you are experiencing.

Knowing the Ropes without Hanging Yourself

*"The only true wisdom is in knowing
you know nothing."*
—Socrates

chapter 5

Studying the Right Way

Surviving in the Pool of Muck and Mire

Now that you have a pretty good idea of what to expect first-year, it is time to let you in on some of the secrets that will make your law school experience easier and less stressful. Certain work that you will be required to perform can actually be enjoyable, depending on the steps that you take to reach your goals. You will not survive in law school without mastering tasks such as researching, briefing, outlining, and, of course, exam-taking. Hopefully, some of the following suggestions will make your job a bit less demanding.

Habitat Habits

Law school starts off in a frenzy. The first few weeks are a confusing blur during which you feel like a hamster on a wheel. You comment continuously about the workload being unimaginable and even ask your classmates—*Is it just me or are these professors deliberately assigning us readings that cannot possibly be completed in the short amount of time between classes?*

Of course, it is not just you. That is why finding all of the shortcuts and study aids early on is so vitally important. However, you have to stop for a moment and recognize when you are not taking care of yourself. You may have made it through college that way, but you are not going to survive the rigors of law school on coffee, little sleep, dirty clothes, and no shower. The bad habits that you formed in college have got to stop. You are working harder, the stress is enormous, the nights are long, the days are longer, the weekends are only for catch-up, you miss your family, and you desperately want a night out with non-law school humans.

EXHIBIT

A second-year student said that in her first year, she walked around most of the time thinking that she had Mononucleosis. She felt so tired and she could never seem to shake it. She said that her schedule was so hectic that she did not even have time to see a doctor. By winter recess, she was forcing herself to get out of bed. She went back home for the break and her mother took one look at her and literally dragged her off for a check-up. She was just completely rundown and suffering from exhaustion. It took awhile for her to gain her strength back, but, after that experience, she made an effort to keep up with her meals, as well as her sleep.

In law school, you do not have time to get sick. You cannot afford to miss a few classes. You do not want to rely on someone else's notes unless it is an absolute emergency. Everybody hears something different in class. What you think is important may be meaningless to others. But you may just be the one who gets it right. In an environment that is filled with people all trying to have the competitive edge, you do not want to fall behind. You need to eat right, exercise, take vitamins, and shower every now and then! Oh, and get some rest.

These are things that you must make a conscious decision to do, because law school can drain you. You need to get off the merry-go-round once in awhile to stop and smell the flowers...as corny and cliché as that sounds. You must take the time to pull yourself back into the real world. Otherwise, you will get so caught up in keeping up that you will find yourself spinning in circles, unable to stop. There are many things that you can do in order to *keep up* without compromising your health. Pay close attention to all of the suggestions in this book and you will stay way ahead of the game.

Researching in the 21st Century

As mentioned earlier, most law schools now provide networks for Internet access. You can bring your laptop and hook right up to the World Wide Web. This eliminates the need for rifling through musty old books in a cold law library until all hours of the night. However, keep in mind that during your first year, most law schools still require you to spend a portion of your time learning the fundamentals of manual research. It is a skill that will carry you through your three years of law school and into your practice of law. If your school offers or mandates researching in the books, take advantage of the opportunity to add something of value to your résumé.

There are several searchable legal databases on the Internet. Many law schools offer students free access to some of the most commonly utilized paid sites, such as LexisNexis and Westlaw, enabling you to gain entrance to them from either school or home. The one drawback is that while becoming proficient in these two wonderful research tools is a requirement, many law schools prohibit the use of them for first-year assignments, a ploy obviously meant to force you to learn how to research the *old fashioned* way.

There are also several free legal sites on the Internet that provide a wealth of information. Some of them include:

- www.alllaw.com;
- www.law.cornell.edu;
- www.findlaw.com; and,
- www.legal-database.com.

There are many more sites to choose from. Most are abundant with links to legal resources that put almost everything you need right at your fingertips. Now, with a click of the mouse, you can perform extensive legal research from home while relaxing in your pj's.

EXHIBIT

One student said that he had first attended law school before the Internet connection was there. He recently returned to the same school for his master's of law, only to happily find that it had finally advanced into the 21st century. He was able to use his laptop to take notes in class, perform research either in the library, around school, or at home, and he could even use it to take his exams. Having experienced research both ways, he said that he only wished he could have spent his three years of law school with this convenient tool. He remembered only too well his long, frustrating, freezing nights in the law library.

Another advantage to researching on the Internet comes after you find what you are looking for—you can cut and paste it right into your documents. It saves an enormous amount of time not to have to write the material freehand or to retype it. You are also generally able to save your place on a site, enabling you to go right back to where you left off. Thus, you do not have to start from the beginning each time you enter the site.

Law students who grew up with the Internet take it for granted. Given the choice to sit in the library or work at home or in their dorm rooms, they choose the obvious. They generally go to the library for some quiet time between classes to do reading assignments or meet friends. But, most of the time, they use the Internet for their work.

That is not to say that the use of law books has become obsolete. Many fine lawyers are still turning pages and using bookmarks. For many tasks, it is still easier to grab a book, look in its table of contents, and immediately find what you are looking for. There is definitely something to be said for the option of convenience.

Reading, Reading, and More Reading

Unlike college texts that are generally meant to teach you something constructive, law school books, referred to as *casebooks*, are filled with cases, otherwise known as decisions of the court that are written by judges and law clerks. Those people are not educators, nor are they in the least bit concerned with the benefits that putting pen to paper might bestow upon a young, curious mind such as yours. The cases are laid down as *precedent* and are mainly meant to be read by other judges, lawyers, law clerks, and the likes, who are already familiar with the legal jargon.

You will find yourself staying up until all hours of the night trying to decipher the meanings of terms that you have yet to come across in your previous life, like *res judicata, collateral estoppel, res ipsa loquitur, escheat, per stirpes, eminent domain,* and *fealty.* Your experience can be compared to that of an elementary school child being given *War and Peace* as a third-grade reading assignment. A number of the words may seem somewhat familiar, but most will not. Even the ones that do jog your memory may not really mean what you think they do. Using your law dictionary will be somewhat helpful for finding the meaning of a term. However, there is no guarantee that you will fully understand what you are reading until your professor puts it into the proper context in class.

At times, pulling a reading together to understand the subject matter will be difficult, because too much time will be spent just trying to translate each new word. When you finally do fully comprehend a reading assignment, new ones may have already been assigned. So, you may occasionally find yourself in a mad rush to keep up.

EXHIBIT

A third-year student said that his first few reading assignments were fairly tedious. He had a hard time understanding how the professors could assign so much material, considering that new students were so disoriented and lost early on. He said that he would sometimes read his assignments over and over, never realizing that the problem was not with him. He began to wonder whether or not he really belonged in law school and only felt somewhat reassured after he overheard other students complaining to each other about the assignments. He said it was comforting to him to learn that he was not alone in his confusion.

Your first assignment may be to read pages 245-372, yes, right smack in the middle of the book. Though it may seem a bit long, you will confidently begin reading. You will move through the pages, somewhat quickly at first, scanning the words, assuming that everything will fall into place shortly. But, you soon begin to feel a slight wave of panic. Nothing is really clicking. You are not sure about anything that you have read and you are already on page 280. You do not understand how that is possible. *How can I be so lost?*

What you are feeling is completely normal. After all, you are not reading stories. The chapters do not flow. There is no plot, no exciting details, and no pattern forming. You may read several cases without even realizing that they are all connected. Due to the profoundly different fact patterns that each case contains, it will be hard at first for you to discern the similarities between them. You will shortly learn that each chapter of your casebook will be comprised of cases that are relevant to a specific topic. You might read about issues such as buying a car, painting a portrait, hiring an employee, ordering ceramic tile, or having a fence painted, and even though they all appear to involve very different types of subject matter, all five cases may be found under the chapter heading "Formation and Termination of Contracts."

Some of the judicial proceedings included within your assignments are common law cases from more than a century ago. There will be no real frame of reference in the back of the book for when you find yourself completely lost in the midst of one hundred year old English. Even though that may actually appear exciting to those of you who are history buffs, imagine reading the following section at 3 a.m. as part of your first law school assignment, prior to setting foot into class. For that matter, imagine reading it at any given time with any amount of preparation:

> *In debt the plaintiff declares upon the lease for years rendering rent at four usual feasts; and for rent behind for three years, ending at the feast of the Annunciation, 21 Car. Brings his action; the defendant pleads, that a certain German prince, by name Prince Rupert, and alien born, enemy to the King and kingdom, had invaded the realm with an hostile army of men; and with the same force did enter upon the defendant's possession, and him expelled, and held out possession from the 19 of July 18 Car. Till the Feast of the Annunciation, 21 Car. Whereby he could not take profits; whereupon the plaintiff demurred, and the plea was resolved insufficient.*
>
> *1. Because the defendant hath not answered to one quarters rent.*
>
> *2. He hath not averred that the army were all aliens, which shall not be intended, and then he hath his remedy against them; and Bacon cited 33 H. 6. 1. E. where the goaler in bar of an escape pleaded, that alien enemies broke the prison &c. And exception taken to it, for that he ought to shew of what countrey they were, viz. Scots, &c.*
>
> *Paradine v. Jane, Hil. 22 Car.Rot. 1178; 82 Eng.Rep. 897. King's Bench, 1647. (Please take note that this was taken directly from the case and that this author did not change the spelling of any of the text.)*

If you read that segment a couple of times, it could begin to make some sense. Maybe. But this is just a speck of sand compared to the vast amount of material that each assignment contains. It is hard to complete all of them, brief them, and understand them, while trying to decipher language similar to the above passage. It is even more difficult to attempt to put the above paragraph into the proper context at the very beginning of a semester, prior to a suitable introduction to the course. Thankfully, most assignments are not as complex. In fact, many are actually comprehensible. But even those are somewhat tedious to complete considering the amount of work you will be assigned. Do what your mother taught you to do; do not think about going out to play until all of your homework is finished. You might not be playing much at first, but, once you get the hang of things, your workload will not seem as heavy.

There are shortcuts that can make law school life much easier, but some are the kind of helpful hints that can cause more harm on a long term basis than you might care to endure. One thing that should not be skimped on is reading your assignments. That is not to say that in a pinch that you should not take a brief respite and use something like a study guide or store-bought outline to help you with your assignments. At times of extreme stress, the only avenue for recourse may be to depend upon commercial outlines. However, there is a lot lost in the translation of those supplements. They are brief and leave out much of the material that you will see while reading the complete text of a case. If you always rely on them, you will never feel fully prepared for a long, drawn out grilling session.

You might ask, "*Since professors hardly ever, in spite of what they say on day one, give credit for class participation, who really cares how badly I fare under the thumb of an uptight Socratic instructor?*" You should care, because by taking shortcuts, you may still make it through law school by the skin of your teeth, but your main goal is not about merely surviving your classroom cross-examinations. It is about being well-prepared for the practice of law. If you take the easy way around assignments on a long-term basis, you are the only one who will lose out in the end.

While you are new to the lingo, find the time to do the actual reading, even if it is at a later date. The more you read your assignments, listen to your professor's lectures, bounce ideas off your peers, and check out the corresponding study aids, the more familiar the terminology will become and the more comfortable you will be with your understanding of the materials put before you. The rewards of your hard work will be obvious later on in your career.

Now that you understand the reasons for reading through difficult assignments, your next task will be to learn how to brief the cases in those assignments in order to better comprehend how they were decided. Thus, in your future practice, you will be equipped to determine how your own cases may play out.

Briefing Briefly

You are sitting comfortably in property class, when your professor startles you by shooting a question your way.

Mr. Smith, state the facts of Pierson v. Post.

You sit there for a moment in silence. You *did* read it last night and you *do* remember that a couple of people were chasing a fox, but you cannot seem to put it into words that make much sense. You stumble around it for awhile, mentioning that there were these two guys chasing a fox and that one got mad at the other for killing it because he was chasing it first and thought it should have belonged to him.

Confused? Well, if you had taken the time to brief the case, you would have been able to give a summary of the facts in a mere two sentences. It would look something like this:

Post pursued a fox through public land, but Pierson caught it, killed it, and collected money for it even though he knew that Post was chasing it first. So, Post sued Pierson.

Briefing simply means creating a very short outline of a case. You root out the most important points and put them into some semblance of order, so you can have all of the facts at your fingertips. It works well for you in the classroom and even better in the courtroom. You do not necessarily have to utilize the prescribed method that your instructors will consistently drill into you. You will most likely develop your own system for recalling facts. Whatever works best for you is what you should use.

Briefing will eliminate some of the humiliation and intimidation that comes from not being thoroughly prepared when it is your turn in the hot seat. You will also gain a much clearer perspective of caselaw. Briefing a case is fairly elementary and it makes answering your professors' questions much more palatable. It also helps you organize your work and better understand all of the different parts that go together to make up a case. When litigating, briefing is essential because judges expect you to make your point as briefly and succinctly as possible.

Unfortunately, by the time a few months of first-year law have passed, many students feel that they understand how to read caselaw well enough to stop briefing. Some of them turn to those previously mentioned *canned briefs* that may be helpful in a jam, but will not replace learning how to dissect a case yourself. The more you practice the fine art of briefing, the better able you will be to understand and argue a case.

At first, briefing is time-consuming and it may seem boring and unnecessary. However, learning how to properly brief a case enables you to get as many facts on the table in as short a time as possible.

The following are the main parts to a brief. Read through each summary to understand how to take a case apart, piece by piece, thereby enabling you to answer any question that your professor might have.

THE PARTIES

The *parties* are the plaintiff and the defendant. They are listed in the heading of the case. The plaintiff is the person who brings the lawsuit against the defendant (e.g. *Pierson v. Post*). However, the first name listed is not always the original plaintiff. By reading the case's *procedural history* (discussed later in this section), you will better understand how a case progressed through the court system.

THE COURT AND DATE

In the heading of the case, you will also find the name of the *court* that adjudicated the case as well as the *date* of adjudication. For example, *Pierson v. Post*, 3 Cai. R. 175, 2 Am. Dec. 264 (Supreme Court of New York 1805).

Also found in the heading is the book that the case is reported in. Here, 3 Cai. R. 175 tells you that in Volume 3 of the Caines' Reports at page 175 you will find this case. *Caines'* is the name of the gentleman who gathered and published the court's opinions two hundred years ago; that was how cases were referenced. Today, cases are gathered in *reporters* that are identified by state or region.

PROCEDURAL HISTORY

The *procedural history* lets you know what has already happened in the case. In *Post v. Pierson*, the trial court judge ruled in favor of Post, saying that he owned the fox because he was in hot pursuit of it when Pierson caught it. Then, Pierson brought suit in the appellate court to overturn the lower court's decision. Thus, you have *Pierson v. Post*. Some jurisdictions maintain the original name of the case as it moves through appellate courts. Others retitle it based on who brings the appeal, as is done in this example.

THE FACTS

The *facts* consist of who is suing whom and why. The facts should be as short as possible to convey what is going on and who is involved. When you first begin briefing, your fact patterns will be too long. Your professor will tell you that, over and over. However, with practice you will be able to sum up ten pages of facts from a case in a couple of sentences.

SPOTTING THE ISSUE

The *issue* is the question before the court. It is the most important part of understanding what you are reading. Unfortunately, there is no shortcut here. The more cases you read, the easier it will be to spot the issue. For example, in *Pierson v. Post*, the issue may be described as, *at what point does a person have a property right in a wild animal?* Issue-spotting is key to being successful both in law school and in your practice of law. Mastering the art of issue-spotting will make your exam-taking experience much more palatable.

THE HOLDING

The *holding* is the court's decision in the case and answers the question asked by the issue. For example, in *Pierson v. Post*, the holding is *mere pursuit of a fox does not constitute ownership.*

STATE THE COURT'S REASONING

Lastly, include what the court relied on in forming its opinion. This includes statutes, precedent-setting decisions, and various other pieces of information.

Now, when your professor shoots a question your way, like, *What is the issue in this case?*—you will be able to respond by simply looking at your notes under the heading *issue.* Any other questions should be easy to answer as well, by using your brief.

Note Taking for Novices

There you sit, pen in hand, awaiting your very first lecture in law school. As in college, you expect the professor to discuss the subject matter in a logical, orderly fashion. You believe that it will flow and you will very shortly gain an accurate perspective of the material. However, when your professor enters the room, the following scene takes place:

She briefly scans the students, stops, turns in your direction, points straight at you and says:

You are an artist. I come to your studio, order a portrait of my grandmother, and promise to pay your fee of $2,500. You paint the portrait and although I agree that it is fantastic, I have since learned that several other artists in my area charge $1,200 for portraits. So I refuse to pay you more than that. You take me to court to sue me for the balance. Will I win?

You sit there, confidently nodding while saying, *Yes.*

The professor then asks, *How can that be?*

You reply, *Well, if I am overcharging you for a service that everyone else performs for less money, then I have no right to win.*

It seems simple enough. It's very clear, black and white, cut and dry. You should not have to pay more for one person's service when everyone else in the area charges significantly less for it. Right?

The professor continues:

Well, then, you walk into a local bakery and see the most beautiful chocolate layer cake that you have ever seen. You usually go to a different local bakery where the chocolate layer cakes are okay and they sell for $7.50. But you would like to try a different bakery and this one charges $11.50. So, do you offer to buy the cake and when the baker hands it to you, do you demand that he only take $7.50 for it? Or, do you make a choice to spend more for what might be a better cake?

You ponder that thought for a moment, realizing that there is a connection between the cake and the portrait. You know that you cannot just walk into a bakery and haggle about their prices or refuse to pay more than what the bakery down the street charges. You are beginning to understand the analogy that your professor has made.

She finishes her point:

Your agreement with the patron to paint the portrait for $2,500 is considered a contract. You have performed your obligation under the contract by painting the portrait. And, the patron has breached her part of the contract by refusing to pay you the *agreed upon price. Thus, I made you an offer, i.e., to pay you $2,500 for the portrait, and you accepted and acted in reliance on the contract by painting the portrait. Unless there is some statute restricting the price of portraits in your state or some other extenuating circumstances, I am obligated to pay you in full for your work.*

What does this have to do with note taking? The above is a typical discussion in a law school contracts class. It is a good demonstration of how a contract is created. The problem is that while the lecture is progressing, you are trying desperately to write down every word that the professor says because you have no idea where she is going to end up. You begin to feel overwhelmed because it is difficult to listen, comprehend, and take notes all at the same time. So you find yourself writing feverishly and yet, you were not really even sure what the point was until the very end of the discussion.

This is where you need to pay attention. In law school, you are going to be taught the core concepts of subjects. In other words, you will learn the basics of how the law is created, how it is utilized, and how issues are resolved. You will also learn what elements are necessary for compliance with the law, as well as what acts are required for a violation to occur. You will learn about statutes and cover such topics as how a contract is formed, how a person's constitutional rights are violated, when civil liability kicks in, what a property interest is, how a will is created, what environmental protections are in place, and many other issues that once you grasp, will stay with you throughout your career. Examples of those issues will be given to you mainly in the form of caselaw. You will read case after case to learn how those types of issues are adjudicated.

Since your lectures will not consist of a topic that has a beginning, a middle, and an ending as they did in college, you cannot simply sit there being spoon-fed notes to throw back at your professor on a final exam. You will be discussing cases made up of facts, elements, rules of law, statutes, policies, and other pieces of legal jargon that fit together to create the important parts of those cases.

Rather than getting caught up in all of the chatter (*i.e.* the non-essential parts of the lecture), it is the wise student who can wade through the unimportant *dicta* and pick out the relevant items that actually belong in your notes.

WHAT TO WRITE

In the very beginning, you will not know what to write down. It takes some time to figure that out. Those first few weeks, when you barely understand anything at all, you will be writing mostly everything down. As time progresses and you read all of your assignments, practice briefing all of the cases, and scan through some of your supplements to get the hang of what the important parts of the cases are, you will start to see that most of the little details that your professor is throwing out at you are not important enough to write down. They are merely examples of the basic premises of law. This is another reason why it will serve you well to do all of your readings and try to outline or brief the cases as best as you can.

As you read, highlight only the things that you deem to be significant regarding what it took to resolve the case at hand. Then, the next day in class, pay close attention to which cases your professor discusses and what points are stressed. While following along with your notes, you can eliminate the ones passed over and asterisk or highlight those parts of the reading focused on. You will soon see the difference between what *you* think is important and what your professor stresses in his or her lectures. This is also a winning strategy for creating your *course outline* (to be discussed next).

Remembering your professor's discussion, think once again about the basic facts that went into the portrait and the cake hypotheticals to determine whether a contract was formed. From that, your notes may reflect the following.

- A contract is a promise that is legally enforceable.
- It is based on *consideration*.
- Consideration is what is offered to a party in return for his or her performance.

- For a contract to exist, there must be an offer from one party and an acceptance from another.
- Once the contract is entered into, if one party does not fulfill his end of the contractual obligation, it is called a breach.

In the portrait *hypothetical*, you are given the core concepts of contract law.

- You have an *offer*, an *acceptance*, and *consideration*.
- The contractual obligation was not met by one of the parties, so, there is a *breach* for which there are remedies under the law.

That is the simple explanation, but it is enough information to help you understand how to take notes on a hypothetical. Had you understood the core concepts of contract law, you would have been better able to answer your professor's question about the portrait, and you would not have wasted your time taking down every single detail.

CUTTING IT DOWN

After getting the hang of note taking, you will not need to write down every word said about contracts in the discussion. It is not a bad idea to jot down a note to remind yourself of the hypothetical when you are first learning about contracts. But the most important part of your notes will be the short, simple explanation of what makes a contract. For example, here is what your notes could look like once you get the hang of it.

Contract = offer + acceptance for consideration.
Breach = not fulfilling contractual obligation.
Hypo: Portrait of grandmother.

You might not be able to make it that simple during class, because you will not necessarily know the end result until the lecture is over. As you begin to fully understand things, you will develop the ability to condense your note taking into brief capsulized versions of what you have heard, especially after briefing the cases and having notes on them already in place for the next day's class. This is not to say that, when taking notes, you should never write more than you need; but the idea is that there are shortcuts that make life a lot easier, and that for those days when you know you wrote too much, you should go home and begin to condense your notes into your *course outline*. This will give you a head start on your outline and will also help reenforce what is necessary to write down.

EXHIBIT

A newly admitted attorney said that she always took notes about the hypotheticals that her professors mentioned because it was easier for her to remember the rules that way. She recalled a hypo about a cheese omelet. Her criminal law professor walked into class one day and began with the following: "Let's compare the law to an omelet recipe. Depending upon how you make your omelet, it could consist of such items as eggs, cheese, ham, onions, mushrooms, salt, and pepper. Now, if you delete or add an item, you will see that the omelet changes. But there are some ingredients that would change the omelet so drastically as to make it into a whole new food.

For example, if you add a pound of pasta, you will change the recipe so much as to now have a pasta dish with eggs. If you omit the eggs, you are again left with no omelet.

The same idea applies to the law. Using criminal law as an example, consider the crime of burglary. If one of the elements is missing, you will not get a conviction on that particular charge. However, you may be able to bring other charges and win a conviction for a different criminal act." The young attorney said that she always thought about that hypothetical when taking an exam, because it reminded her how to determine whether or not the proper elements existed for a case to prevail.

You are probably asking yourself once again what this has to do with note taking. Hopefully, you will be able to recognize the analogy between the omelet recipe and what you should take down in your notes. Suppose your professor is lecturing about a recipe for an omelet. By now, you should understand the need to simply write something like—

Omelet = eggs, cheese, ham, onions, mushrooms, salt, pepper.

Then, you could make note of how the omelet could be changed into something else depending upon those ingredients—

Eggs missing, no omelet.
Add pasta, no longer omelet, but now, possibly pasta dish.

The importance of this is that as the ingredients, or *elements* change, so does the recipe, or *charges, legal implications, policy issues,* and *outcome.* In your notes, you only need to write down those elements and the possible outcome. You would not need to get into the whole discussion of how you have to break the eggs, slice the cheese, chop the ham, dice the onions, etc. Those are the things that you will keep in the back of your mind and recall when reading the simple notes that you have taken. If you are discussing criminal law, you need only list the elements of a crime and, perhaps, a case or hypo as an example to remember. You may also want to jot down some mitigating circumstances that would change the scenario or maybe take note of a missing element. These are the types of shortcuts that are valuable to you and do not shortchange you in the long run. Every time you learn a method to make your day a little easier, you make your law school experience that much more palatable.

SHORT CUTS

There are other shortcuts to use during note taking. Certain words can be abbreviated to enable you to write more quickly. A few of the more common ones follow.

- Δ = Defendant
- D = Defendant
- π = Plaintiff
- P = Plaintiff
- Ct. = Court
- JM = Judgment
- K = Contract
- SJ = Summary Judgment
- H = Holding

Of course, you have already gone through college and you may have developed your own system for note taking. Use any method that works best for you. As you will soon see, it is vitally important to find ways to make note taking easier to handle.

Recording Rhetoric

There are those who carry around mini tape recorders for the purpose of catching every word said in class. Other uses include asking classmates to tape lectures when you cannot attend. It is always a good back-up to have a class taped for a day when you cannot be there and something of vital importance is discussed. However, the majority opinion on this subject is that there is barely enough time to get your assignments completed; finding a couple of extra hours in the day to listen to a garbled tape recording is not going to be an easy task or a practical replacement for a missed class.

A better suggestion is to get someone else's notes. Do not simply look to one of your buddies. Find a student who stands out in class as far as intelligent participation is concerned and see if he or she is willing to share notes. When you receive the notes, take a close look at which cases your professor discussed, so you will be on track with the significance of the lesson. If you have not already done so, read them and brief them.

> **NOTE:** It helps to pre-arrange getting someone else's notes because, when people know they are taking notes for others, they generally make the effort to give you something more legible and coherent than if they were merely doing it for themselves.

Outlining for Success

Outlines are essential for successful exam taking. The size of the law school workload is such that there is no way to retain everything in your head. There is also no possible way to study the hundreds of pages of an entire semester's notes when exam time nears. As mentioned earlier, a well-prepared outline is simply an abbreviated version of your course's class notes. You edit them by selecting the most significant material while eliminating useless dicta. This is more easily done by taking your class notes on a laptop. However, if you prefer pen and paper, you can also transpose your notes each day or at the end of each week onto your computer or laptop at home. This, unfortunately, can take time away from other important work that needs to be done. Either way, you will definitely need to have an outline for exam purposes.

A well-prepared outline should contain all of the topics covered in class. However, remember to pay special attention to the topics that your professors focus on. Those are the subject areas that you will probably see on your exams. Under each topic you will list all of the essential elements pertaining to the topic. For example, if you are working on contract law, you might want your outline to include the following:

Contract = Offer + Acceptance for consideration
          (i.e. Portrait of grandmother)

Of course, this is extremely simplified, but the point is that you can now recall all of the details of the portrait case, so you do not need to write it all down in your outline. If you are given a question on your exam regarding a contract, you will look for the offer, the acceptance, the consideration, and the breach. You may think about the portrait case to compare it to the case at hand. You might be given a case about the services of a hairdresser or the sale of a car. The basic elements of the contract will still be the same.

The main reason for the outline is that, unlike college, where you had midterms, finals, and possibly a few quizzes in between, in law school most of your exams will be taken at the end of the semester. Generally, there will be no midterm, unless it is the rarely seen practice exam. This means that your grade for the entire semester depends on what you can spew forth in a relatively short period of time on one stressful morning. Also, grading is often based on a curve, so not only must you do well, but perform better than the person sitting next to you. How high your grades are depends on how well each student does. As unfair as that may seem, it is the way that law school determines your class status. You must be able to perform well and efficiently, especially under extreme pressure.

In spite of what you may hear in law school, there are many methods for outlining and you should find one that works best for you. Often, there will be student-made outlines circulating that were created by others who took the same courses with the same professors as you. Those are the most valuable. They will look familiar because your professors generally stay close to the same curriculum from one semester to the next. They are extremely helpful because, depending upon how detailed they are and how closely they resemble your own semester's syllabus, they will be saving you many hours of tedious work. You will be able to recognize solid outlines because they will be well-organized, easy to follow, and the subject matter will flow, unlike your semester-long course. Knowing who prepared the outline or who is passing it on will also be an indication of how helpful it will be. Of course, what is good for someone else is not necessarily good for you. Compare it to your own notes to make sure the material correlates, is understandable, and is helpful to you.

EXHIBIT

One attorney said that he had made his mind up early on that he was not going to prepare his own outlines. He said that he tried it once and it did not take long for him to realize that he just was not that good at it and that it was too time-consuming with all of his other commitments. Instead, he made it his business to ferret out the best outlines circulating around his school. He never failed to obtain them and had a vast collection by the end of third-year. He was careful to accept outlines only from those students who not only had the same courses with the same professors, but who also had a reputation for excelling. The outlines did him justice—his grades were excellent. Of course, he passed the outlines on to others.

These hand-me-down outlines serve three important purposes. First, they are great to follow along with in class from as early as the first day, if possible; second, they are very helpful guides for preparing your own outlines and studying for exams; and third, they are wonderful stand-ins for those times when you are just too inundated with work to prepare your own.

chapter 6

Strategic Exam Taking

The Truth about Law School Exams

Whatever you have heard about law school exams is all true. They are generally given only at the end of each semester and they are always difficult. They are often comprised of hypothetical fact patterns meant to slightly resemble some of the cases that you read throughout the course. There will almost always be time and page limits and you will inevitably leave the exam room feeling completely drained. Your entire grade for each course depends on one exam, and if you want to pass, you will spend every waking moment all semester preparing for it.

There are a couple of familiar scenarios that come to mind when thinking of law school finals. Both are disastrous and both need to be discussed.

Scenario #1: It's two o'clock in the morning and you have your contracts final in six hours. It's been a long semester and you are just about burnt out. You have not had time to keep up with your work during the semester, but you did open your books for an hour or so earlier in the evening. Your plan is to drink lots of coffee and stay up studying until exam time, just like you did in college.

Scenario #2: You arrive at your assigned exam room and find a seat. The proctor hands out the exams and tells you exactly how much time you have to finish. You begin reading the first fact pattern. It is long and complicated. You recognize some of the material from a case you read, but there are twists that are completely unfamiliar to you. You become a bit stressed and go back to reread the fact pattern. You start thinking about an answer, but you are not really sure what the question is yet. You begin writing. You write and write and keep on writing, but you continue thinking of new ideas, and each time you do, you start over. You fill up exam book after exam book, feeling as though you are getting nowhere fast. You have not even moved on to question two and the first hour has already gone by. You panic. Your mind goes blank. You know that you cannot finish the exam, and you feel as though the situation is hopeless.

There is a huge difference between the way that you prepared for college exams and what is necessary to tackle those in law school. Law school exams are not like any other test that you have ever taken. In college, your exams were mainly comprised of questions that you were able to answer by merely regurgitating what you had learned in class. In law school, your lessons are meant to teach you how to think. You are expected to master your analyzing and reasoning skills as well as your ability to be objective.

As you know by now, the cases that you are assigned to read are simply examples to demonstrate how the law is created. You are not expected to memorize them. However, you will be required to understand how jurists came to their conclusions called the *holding* of the case. While reading your assignments, you are expected to look beneath the facts and understand the reasoning, the policy issues, the arguments, and finally, the outcome. Thus, when you are faced with a case in the exam room, you cannot simply spit back the lessons as in college. You must think, analyze, and bring your ideas to a reasonable conclusion.

The purpose of this training becomes quite clear after awhile. When you practice law, with each case that you take on, you will be required to listen carefully to your clients and try to give them some indication of possible outcomes. In order to properly do that, you must understand how to compare the case at hand to the cases that have already been adjudicated. Most often, your cases will not be exactly like the ones that you read about in school or thereafter, and you will be required to come up with your own strategies and arguments in support of your position. Each case is unique and requires serious analytical thought.

When you take your exam, you must use what you have learned to analyze the hypothetical fact patterns that you are given. It takes great skill to craftily dissect a situation and come up with all sides of an issue. You must be able to determine what each of the issues are and what outcomes are possible.

As an attorney, you will be trying to determine whether a case is a winner or whether there is nothing that can be done. Of course, you will be wrong sometimes. You may let a case go only to read about it in the papers in the near future and see the prevailing attorney all over the news. It happens to everyone.

Attorneys are not magicians. They can only do their best. They cannot always anticipate what will happen, and they may actually even win a case by default. They may also win a case because they came up with an angle that nobody else thought of or that is just too good to dispute. Sometimes, they may prevail because the judge had a bad day and the other attorney was rubbing him or her the wrong way.

For the most part, they will win by being well-prepared. That also applies to law school exams. You must learn the ropes that will last you a lifetime in order to survive this one stressful day.

Tricks of the Trade

The following are some quick tricks for exam success. You may have heard them before, but they bear repeating.

Read your assignments and brief your cases.
During an exam, you will most definitely be faced with fact patterns that resemble your readings. They will not be quite the

same, and they will always leave you in somewhat of a quandary for at least a small amount of time. This is why it is so important to understand how to take a case apart and analyze every detail. Even though there is always going to be an argument for each side, only the best and most well-thought out argument wins. Do not skimp on your assignments. Learn the corresponding laws and policies behind the holdings, and understand how the conclusions were developed. You will be expected to do that on your law school exams, as well as on the all-important bar exam.

Keep track of which cases your professor focuses on.

There will be many discussions in class where students bring up cases they read as part of the assignments. It is not important to remember what your fellow classmates discuss. Your professor has a specific curriculum to follow and it will not change based upon what students bring up in class. So unless one of your classmates says something so profound that the professor commends the point and expounds upon it at length, do not waste time putting it into your notes. Those notes will be transformed into your outline; you do not want anything in there that is not relevant to what will be asked on your exams.

Use past exams for practice.

Most law school professors keep their old exams on file to help students get an idea of how they will be tested. This is especially helpful for first-year students who have never seen a law school exam before. Find out as early as possible if those exams exist and where they can be found. Some law schools have them on file in the library and/or posted online on the school website.

Often, a professor who has been teaching a specific subject for an extended period of time covers the same material from one semester to the next. It is not uncommon to discover that many of their exam questions are repeated every couple of semesters. They may not be word for word, but they will have a similar fact pattern, and the professor will be looking for the same type of answers. Either way, reading past test questions and writing practice answers is an excellent way to prepare for exams.

Allocate your time.

Most exams are made up of two, three, or four essay questions, depending upon how many credit hours of class time took place. For example, if the credits to be earned are two, you may have a two-hour exam. If there are three credits, the time may extend to three hours, and so on. Sometimes, there will be short answer or multiple choice questions, but for the most part, you will be writing essays.

There are time and page limits on exams to help you construct brief and coherent answers. It is very important that you understand how to allot your time appropriately in order to properly answer your essay questions. Once you know how many hours and how many questions you have been given, allocate your time. For example, on a three hour exam, if equal weight is given to each essay and you divide your time accordingly, you will have one hour to read, outline, and complete each answer.

It will probably take at least twenty minutes to read the fact pattern. This leaves only forty minutes to write. As you can see, you will be pressed for time. You have forty minutes to outline and write an answer that is one-third of an entire semester's grade. You need to carefully adhere to your time allotment for each answer. When you use it up, you must move on to the next essay. If you have time left at the end, you can go back to finish an uncompleted answer. Never go past your allotted time the first time around.

The first thing to do is find the question being asked.

It is always a good idea to go to the end of the fact pattern right away to see exactly what is being asked of you. Then, while reading through the fact pattern, it is easier to recognize the specific issues that are relevant to the question.

Read and reread the fact pattern.

When looking over your exam, take your time, breathe deeply, relax, and read through the first fact pattern. Do not attempt to write anything until you have started reading it a second time. Then, underline important facts, jot notes in the margins, and use your scrap paper to write down significant points or issues that stand out. These notes will be the basis for your answer. Be careful and remain calm. There is enough time if you do not waste it by panicking.

Spot the issues.

As you will learn long before preparing for exams, you must know how to spot the issue, identify the rule, analyze what you have, and then come to your conclusion. This is known in many circles as the *IRAC* (Issue, Rule, Analysis, and Conclusion) method. It is merely a simplified way to view your task. But it does clarify what you must ultimately do on your exam, as well as in your practice of law.

Of course, practicing law is not as clear-cut and simple as this sounds. The rules do not apply to every situation, and it is a fact that judges and juries do not always decide in your favor, even when you are sure that you will prevail. Nothing is black and white in the law. There are shortcuts and loopholes and mitigating circumstances. Thus, when taking your exam, you may come to more than one conclusion for an answer. You must simply decide which is the best one, frame it out, and write clearly and precisely. If you have time, you can always add, *If the judge decides that there are no grounds for that charge...* or whatever is relevant to your essay, and give the opposing view. Hopefully, you have not missed an important point that totally negates one of your arguments.

IRAC

Issue spotting is simple. While reading the fact pattern, you will need to stay focused. There will be so many facts that you may stare blankly at the page trying to figure out what to do first. If you arrive well-prepared, knowing what the rules of law are, something should click. Once it does, begin jotting down notes on your scrap paper. Using IRAC, try to briefly outline what you think the answer will be. You may find that the fact pattern, depending on certain items, results in conflicting situations. Even though your analysis may leave the possibility for different conclusions, the issues will still stand out. An example of this is the following brief hypothetical, otherwise known as the *fact pattern*.

> Kevin was arrested for burglary after he was caught climbing in through the window of a house. The owners were out of town and a neighbor saw him enter. At the police station, Kevin insisted that his brother, Richard, lived in the house, that he had told Richard he would be away in Europe for a long time and that he had arrived home unexpectedly. However, there was a problem with his story because his keys did not fit the door lock, his brother did not live there, and his identification listed his address as being different from the house. Thus, the police officer booked him.

How do you develop an answer? Use *IRAC*.

Issue

Assuming that you attended your criminal law class with some degree of regularity, you would recognize that the issue is *whether or not Kevin committed the crime of burglary.*

Rule

The rule from the fact pattern is as follows:

The elements necessary for a finding of burglary, depending upon the jurisdiction, are *the breaking and entering into a dwelling or place of business with the intent to commit a crime therein*.

The fact pattern *appears* to describe the elements of the crime of burglary.

NOTE: Keep in mind as we move along that the most important element here is *intent*. This means that if Kevin went in through the window for any other reason besides committing a crime, he cannot be charged with burglary. That is not to say that he cannot be charged with any crime, such as trespass. But, for our purposes, we are just analyzing burglary.

Analysis

This is where you put the facts to the test. Your analysis should determine whether or not the charge of burglary is appropriate in regard to the rule. You begin by looking at each fact separately.

Fact #1

If Kevin had actually lived in that house with his brother, Richard, he might have a valid defense.

Fact #2

However, if Kevin had lived with Richard, but was evicted or purposefully moved out while Richard still lived there, he might have no valid defense.

So, the following questions must be asked to determine what position a defense attorney might take on the burglary charge.

Can Kevin prove that he actually resided in the house with Richard?

For example:

Does he have any type of lease, written, or verbal agreement? Has Richard acknowledged that he and Kevin resided there before Kevin left for Europe?

- If Kevin can prove that he lived there with Richard, it may remove the *intent to commit a crime* element.

If Richard did live in the house, did he continue residing there after Kevin left?

For example:

Did Richard move out before or after Kevin left?

- If it is proven that Richard moved out prior to Kevin's departure, and Kevin was not a legal owner of the premises or that he had no lease, then, the assumption would be that Kevin was aware that he had no legal basis for climbing in through the window.

Did Richard move out of the house while Kevin was out of the country?

For example:

Was there anything to indicate that Kevin had been notified that Richard moved?

- If it can be proven that Kevin knew that Richard had moved and Kevin had no legal right to the premises on his own, then again, the assumption would be that Kevin was aware that he had no legal basis for climbing in through the window.

Was there any indication when Kevin arrived at the house that someone new had moved in?

For example:

Was there a sign on the house that had the new occupant's name on it?

- If Kevin had arrived at the house and there was a sign in plain view that read, "The Smith Family Welcomes You," then, it is reasonable to assume that Kevin knew that he should not enter the house through the window without first investigating who the Smith's were.

The answers to the above questions all make a difference regarding the outcome of the case against Kevin.

Conclusion

At trial, Kevin's attorney presented evidence that Richard had, in fact, previously leased that house and that Kevin had lived there prior to leaving for Europe. He also proved that Kevin had moved into the house just before leaving on his business trip and that Richard had continued to reside there for some time thereafter. Due to Kevin's undercover work, he was unable to communicate with Richard for several months and they lost touch. In the interim, due to a job transfer, Richard broke the lease and moved. Subsequently, new tenants took possession of the house, but did not put out any sign on the property indicating that anyone new had moved in.

Thus, the facts prove the following:

- Kevin had resided in the house with Richard, who held a valid lease.
- Kevin moved away while Richard was still residing there.
- Kevin lost touch with his brother before his brother vacated the premises.

Therefore, it is reasonable to assume that Kevin climbed in through the window thinking that it was still Richard's home.

- The requisite *intent to commit a crime therein* was not present.
- There are no grounds for a conviction on the charge of burglary.

This is a valuable demonstration that even though the facts appeared to be clear, the necessary elements for a finding of burglary were not present. While spotting issues and framing an answer, be careful not to jump to quick conclusions prior to thoroughly analyzing all of the facts. There may be more than one possible outcome. Discuss all of them.

Outline your answers.

Just as you will learn to properly outline your class notes, you must also master the art of outlining exam answers. You begin the process by jotting down notes along the margins as you read through the fact pattern. You may spot a policy issue, an element of a crime, a question of jurisdiction, or any one of a number of important details that will be relevant to your answer. Once you have jotted down all of the details that you recognize, begin outlining your answer.

Outlining an answer is similar to outlining a paper. You try to coordinate it so that your answer is clear and well-organized. This is where *IRAC* is helpful. Write down the issue, your rule, and notes regarding your analysis. Then, you will hopefully have a good idea what your conclusion will be. There does not need to be a lot of writing. You should just be framing out a guide to follow to write your essay.

It is important to take your time and not to begin writing without following the steps as explained. Otherwise, you may find yourself going in circles, repeating yourself, or losing track.

Be brief.

If you were foolish enough to jot down every single word spoken in class, you have your work cut out for you. Law school is a very structured environment and the professors are generally very busy people. Most have various other things keeping them occupied outside of the classroom. They may be working on a book or an article, have committees to chair, or projects to organize. The point is that they do not want to spend several hours poring over exam answers. They simply want to know that you understand how to untangle and analyze the law. This is one place where the more you write, the worse it is. This is why there are page limits. Do not assume that you can pass the limit and it will not matter. Many professors make it clear that if the page limit is six and you write seven, that last page will not be read.

The page limit serves more than one purpose. While professors do not have all the time in the world to read hundreds of pages of essay answers, neither do judges. The sooner you learn how to put down your thoughts clearly and briefly, the better off you will be. Nobody wants to read pages of fluff or fill. Get to the point as quickly and succinctly as possible.

Remember, this is the time when you want your answer to be brief, because it is not about how much you write, but about how much substance you write in the least amount of space. Quality versus quantity!

Stick to the point.

Stay with the question being asked. If you are asked only about the crime of burglary and not what crimes you think could have been committed, do not waste time going into the other possibilities. While it might be a nice demonstration of your knowledge, professors are more impressed when you follow their instructions and stay on point than if you go all over the place.

Stay calm.

This is easier than it sounds. You have to put things into the proper perspective. You are in school taking an exam and you do know the work. Everything really rests on how calm you can remain during the height of a storm. Many people walk into the exam room and let their thoughts run wild.

This is the most important day of my life.

If I fail this test, I fail the whole course and my life will be over.

How can I possibly do better than that kid who sits in front of me?

What if I don't recognize anything at all on the exam?

What if I run out of time?

The truth is, everyone panics a little before their exams. Self-doubt runs rampant in law school during finals week. Those feelings are nonproductive—all they will do for you is make you waste valuable time. You made it through college. You were accepted into law school. You are a pretty smart person. Keep your chin up and just do your best.

It may seem a bit too simple to think that having a system is the answer to conquering your exams. You might be getting the impression that once you master a system, you will have it made in law school. However, what you need to realize right up front is that this *system* is not about tricks and magic. It is about hard work and good exam-taking strategies. There is no quick fix in law school. The best advice that anyone can give you is to keep up with your workload and study hard. Having a plan of action to carry with you into the exam room is the key to staying calm and keeping your feet on the ground in a tense situation.

Passing is Not Enough

There is another truth about law school: it really does not take all that much effort to pass an exam. Of course, your goal is not just to pass it, but to excel. The secret to excelling is in having a strategy to tackle the entire test. Bombing completely and flunking out is not likely to happen. There is no way to sit through an entire semester, read your assignments, brief your cases, attend classes, and participate in discussions without absorbing the most important aspects of each course. You may not realize it yet, but once you open the exam, you will see that you know more than you think. The worst thing that might happen is that you have not learned any strategies for writing a clear and logical answer. But, at least you will have written something down, and as incoherent as it may be, if there is any connection at all to the exam question, you will receive some credit. Most people do not flunk out of law school. The ones who do, fail because they treat it as though they were still in college and slack off until the last minute. They do not keep up with their assignments, and they assume they can play catch up as they had previously. They cannot. If you remember that, you will be much more relaxed about exams.

There is no doubt that law school exams and stress are synonymous, but the anticipation is much worse than the reality. If you have done your job and you find that when you open your exam, you recognize very little, then the odds are that everyone else feels the same way.

EXHIBIT

A recent law graduate said that when she began taking her last law school final, she couldn't believe her eyes. She was a good student and had kept up with her assignments. She had performed adequately on all of her other exams, but when she opened this one, she was horrified. Most of the subject matter was unfamiliar. She sat there staring at the fact patterns and soon realized that there was nothing she could do. As she looked around the room, she realized that she was not alone. Everyone was obviously bewildered. People began asking the proctors for guidance. The proctors were clueless. The students were upset. Time passed and one by one, people began writing, but they were really not sure what they were writing about. When the exam ended, students frantically left the room in search of the professor. Since the entire class had not only complained, but had performed inadequately, there was no choice but to put a huge curve on the exam.

That wonderful curve can bring everyone's grades up when an exam is more difficult than it was meant to be. Just because those around you are writing while you stare at an exam, that does not necessarily mean they know more than you. It just means that they have found a place to begin. You will too and once you do, you will see that it will all come back to you. If it does not, you will not be alone. If you do find yourself stuck during an exam, simply make a list of all of the elements of the crime, policy issues, rules of law, or whatever is relevant to the subject matter and you will almost certainly earn some credit (especially on the bar exam).

Anonymity

Law school grading is anonymous. Students are assigned individual numbers that allow professors to grade exams without knowing the identity of the test-taker. Accordingly, this system also permits students to obtain posted grades without everyone else knowing to whom the grade belongs. For those of you who have felt as though you bombed due to poor class participation or for rubbing a professor the wrong way, do not spend too much time stressing out over it. More than likely, that is not the case. Your professor should only see the correlation between you and your exam grade after the grades are recorded. They are then given the opportunity to change the grade a small degree depending on their policies for grading (*i.e.*, if they do happen to give credit for class participation). However, if you do think you have been graded unfairly, your school will have avenues for recourse.

Using Your Laptop

In many schools, you now have the option of taking your exams on your laptop. In schools allowing for this feature, a certain number of exam rooms are set aside specifically for that purpose. Generally, security-enhanced software is provided that allows you to take the exam while, at the same time, preventing access to any of your own laptop files. Certain restrictions may apply regarding the number of students permitted to take the exam on laptop, the type of equipment necessary, deadlines for permission, as well as what to expect if your laptop crashes during the exam.

If you are well-versed in computers, use your laptop. If not, be sure that you know all of the ins and outs of it and the exam software before you choose your laptop as your method for exam taking.

The decision to take an exam on your laptop is a personal one and should not be made by listening to what others feel about it. If you consider utilizing your laptop, it might be wise to discuss it with the information specialist or computer technician at your school to find out what is involved and what possible glitches could occur. Be prepared to deal with any problems that may arise and what the likely solutions will be, so you do not find yourself in a panic-stricken state on that all-important exam day.

SECTION 4

Second Year

A moment's insight is sometimes worth a life's experience.
—Oliver Wendell Holmes

chapter 7

Freedom to Choose

Loosening the Leash
to Determine Your Own Path

Now that you made it through first-year, you can breathe a bit easier. First-year is generally viewed as the test. Attending law school is pretty much like starting your life over from scratch, and it is somewhat reassuring when you realize that everyone else is on the same footing—lost. It feels as though you have wandered into a strange, new world without being able to communicate with the natives. As time passes, a few words become more familiar, and just as the year comes to a close, you actually think you can understand the inhabitants enough to settle down and stay for awhile. There is a long-held belief that if you are able to survive your first year, the odds are very much in your favor that you will make it all the way to graduation. As a matter of fact, it is hard to believe that someone could successfully complete first-year and not, barring any unforeseen tragedy, graduate.

Unlike first-year, you are now given the opportunity to choose many of your classes. Most law schools have some second-year requirements that must be fulfilled. Those may include such subjects as constitutional law, ethics, and legal research and writing. But there is still room for flexibility in your schedule. Depending on how you arrange your course load, your second year may be much more palatable than your first. The course selection guide will generally be diverse enough to allow you to experience various areas of law. You should make every effort to register for courses that are closely related to your specific areas of interest, as well as those that may be an asset to you on the bar exam.

In second-year, you will also have more time to participate in activities that did not fit into your first-year program. Life will seem more like it did in college. You have become more accustomed to your new environment and are better equipped to handle situations that caused stress for you during first-year. If you were smart enough to take the suggestions in this book to prepare for first-year, imagine how much easier second-year will seem compared to your shell-shocked classmates who are still reeling from the stress of their surroundings.

By now, you have been given enough information to survive first-year. It is time to discuss several strategies that will help to make the following two years as successful as possible. Since you now know that you can prepare ahead of time for what to expect at the end of a semester, use that to your advantage. Every little thing that you are able to do to accentuate your strengths will help to make your law school experience a success. That is why it is important to take advantage of your opportunity to do more than merely prepare for finals.

The best chance that you have to excel in law school is to select your courses carefully and with great skill. You must choose them after evaluating elements other than just the subject matter. That is not to say that you should not choose any courses based on their content—of course you should. In law school, you have to be more creative when putting together a workable schedule. In order to succeed against the fierce competition, you must choose classes that will give you the best possible chance of excelling. This may sound somewhat simplistic considering that you tried to do that in college. However, this recommendation is geared towards working the system to your advantage. The following suggestions will guide you to do that.

Get to Know Your Professors
Before You are in Their Classes

It is the wise student who chooses not only the courses that seem advantageous, but also the professors who will help make the experience the most beneficial. Once you have tackled first-year law, you are reasonably familiar with many professors. You may have even developed a few relationships. Those relationships will prove to be quite useful during your next two years. You might find yourself in a position where there are no courses that fit your particular needs, so you may consider registering for an independent study. Or, you may feel that you have the extra time necessary to become a professor's research assistant. Whatever the case, the many advantages of being on familiar terms with professors will become obvious while you are perusing course selections for next semester.

As you probably learned during college, the professors' personalities, as well as their particular methods of instruction and grading, have a lot to do with your success or failure in a course. There are many things to consider when choosing your schedule including the following items.

- The method the professor utilizes in teaching the course (*i.e.*, Socratic). *Decide whether you are able to thrive under that type of instruction.*
- The type of personality the professor has and whether you are comfortable with it. *Is the professor a hard-nosed pedagogue who does not engage in discussion during class, but sticks to a specific agenda without any diversions?*
- Does the professor randomly call on students or is there a system that you can count on to determine when your participation will be required?
- Is the professor responsive to questions and concerns, both inside and outside of the classroom?
- Does the professor gives credit for class participation? *Most of the time, class participation has no bearing on grades. However, professors tend to tell you that it will in order to make you feel the*

need to readily offer answers. Occasionally, you will hear of a professor who actually does give some credit.

How does a professor react when you are unprepared?

- *Sometimes the humiliation is worse than not getting credit for regular participation.*
- Whether the professor assigns papers, administers exams, or allows for the option of either. *If exams are given, it is important to know whether there will be just one end-of-the-semester final or more exams during the term. (The general rule is that law school professors are famous for giving only one final exam and no others.) It is also important to know if the exams are open- or closed-book. Is there a paper option? (Since professors expect you to be prepared for every class, it can be more burdensome to add on the extra responsibility of a paper.)*
- The grading system the professor utilizes. *By now, you know what strengths and weaknesses you have in particular areas; you should be prepared to choose which method of grading you prefer. (There are pass/fails where no grade is given. This is one way to avoid bringing down your GPA.)*
- The most important feature to investigate is the professor's reputation regarding how tough he or she is on grading. *There are professors who habitually administer unfavorable grades to students.*

Another method for choosing professors utilized at some law schools is to have student-created course evaluations posted online so that others are given insight into which professors would suit them best.

For example, one school lists the following student critique. *Professor Smith is well-organized, funny, and quite interesting. He is straightforward in his lectures and generally informs students ahead of time when they will be called upon in class. His reading assignments are doable and he spends most of his class time covering only those materials that will be specifically addressed on the exam. His exams are open-book and he has several previous ones on file in the library. Study them and you will do well. Occasionally, if a student has a valid reason for the request, he will allow for the option of doing a paper instead of an exam.*

Grading Methods

As you look over the list of professors, seriously think about the suggestions mentioned regarding each one's grading methods. At this point in your education, you know to what extent your exam-taking skills will work to your advantage. Consider that when deciding which courses to choose. You will experience both open-book and closed-book exams. Before choosing courses based on the type of tests that you desire, you should examine the pros and cons of each.

OPEN-BOOK EXAMS

When taking an open-book exam, it is not uncommon to bring in too much material and get lost under the overwhelming pile of papers.

EXHIBIT

An attorney described his civil procedure exam. His professor, characterized as an undeniably brilliant man, was teaching at his law school for the first time and soon became famous for his never-ending handouts. The final exam was open-book, so students were allowed to bring in all of their class materials, including any outlines they had prepared. When the students entered the exam room, the proctors had a hard time accepting that the unbelievably huge pile of papers and books they were carrying all came from that one course. Of course, bringing so many materials to a test was something he said they all learned was a huge mistake, but not before they struggled through the exam.

Sometimes, it is not the amount of papers that are a hindrance.

EXHIBIT

A recently admitted attorney had opted for a limited open-book exam during second-year. This meant that she was permitted to bring into the exam room as much material as she could fit onto one sheet of paper. Thinking she was pretty slick, she changed the font on her computer to enable her to fit almost an entire semester's outline on that one sheet while others agonized over the limited amount of material that they had with them. The exam began and, looking to her sheet of notes, she thought it would be a piece of cake. Unfortunately, the print was so tiny that she could hardly read it. The result was that she could not find anything she needed and she suffered from eye strain long before the exam ended.

It is apparent that the students who entered the exam room with the small amount of material had studied much harder than the one with the entire outline on a single sheet of paper. If you prepare properly, it does not matter what you bring to the exam. In an open-book test situation, the right materials will be beneficial to you. You must condense the most important information and have it organized in a way that enables you to locate what you need at any given time. You may even find that bringing a very brief student-prepared outline is best for you.

If you know your material, then just having a frame of reference will be helpful. Bringing in the rules of law and nothing else may work well for some students. In the end, if you do not know your material, you can bring in every note, casebook, and outline that you have and it will be useless to you. You must decide whether or not you are equipped to take an open-book exam with the proper materials, knowing that no matter what you are allowed to carry into the exam room, the only way you are going to pass is to be fully capable of thinking on your feet, as you will be required to do as an attorney.

Closed-book exams

A closed-book exam, where you must know your material by heart, can also be difficult, depending upon how well you hold up under stress. However, these exams are not as bad as they seem. Some students are champion test takers, they recognize that their strengths lie in their ability to properly prepare for what others see as gut-wrenching moments. Preparing properly includes learning the basic elements of each law course. Unfortunately, many students get caught up in all of the dicta and forget the simple details that create the basic foundation for each type of law.

Using the burglary example from Chapter 6, think about what these rules can mean to you during an exam. Assume that you are given the fact pattern about Kevin climbing into the window of a house. If you were equipped in the exam room with your notes and an outline, how would you handle the facts? While rifling through your materials, hopefully, you would know better than to search for the exact same fact pattern under the assumption that you could merely copy the case right into your test booklet. It will not happen. The exams are purposefully created to make you think. Consider what you already know about the crime of burglary. What elements constitute the crime of burglary? As you read through the fact pattern, the elements should look familiar.

You will begin by listing those elements. Then, you will jot down the bare facts of the case. As you move through the *IRAC* system and attempt to determine whether there is enough evidence to prove that Kevin committed a crime, things should fall into place. In the end, you will realize that there was really nothing that you had the need to search through your notes for except maybe to reassure yourself about the elements of burglary.

This is really a simple case for the memorization of basic rules and elements that will apply to many situations. If your hypothetical is about a man climbing in through a store window or breaking the lock on the back door of a liquor store and entering, you should automatically recall Kevin. You should also think about all of the mitigating circumstances that could alter the charges. Consider the cheese omelet and remember that one small change in the recipe can modify the entire outcome. When you know the basics, you will be able to tackle even the most unfamiliar hypothetical.

Whether you choose open- or closed-book exams, expect the unexpected and do not underestimate the power of learning the fundamentals that constitute the core ingredients in each course. The most important feature of your law school education will be the fact that your professors have one common goal and that is to make you use your brain. Once you are an attorney, you will be grateful for those grueling sessions where you had to actually think rather than regurgitate back what your professors gave you.

PAPER PEDAGOGY

Writing a paper has many advantages over taking exams. While it is still necessary to keep up with your assignments and be prepared for class, you do have some room to slack off a bit when you are not worrying about taking a final exam. For example, you do not have to prepare an outline, studying is not necessary, and paper deadlines stretch out over the semester, leaving you some breathing room.

The final bonus to writing a paper is the reduced stress level. There is nothing more anxiety-producing than taking one final exam that your entire semester's grade rests on. The paper, with the aid of your professor's guidance, will become a polished work of art by the end of the term, thereby allowing you the best opportunity for an excellent grade.

Other Important Questions

Once you have determined which professors are the most desirable and you have thought about the pros and cons of open- and closed-book exams and paper courses, there are a few other details to ponder before creating your schedule.

What subject areas truly interest you?
Even if a professor has everything else that makes a course palatable, you must still have some interest in the subject matter in order to do fairly well.

EXHIBIT

A third-year student said that even though it was not a requirement, she registered for a tax course. She had the professor for another class and truly enjoyed the experience. Unfortunately, the course bored her to tears. She struggled through it and did not perform terribly, but she said the grade was not nearly as bad as having to spend the entire semester in that class.

Are you a strong enough writer to make writing a paper the better choice over taking an exam?
This is a touchy issue. As you now know, law school writing and college writing are completely foreign to each other. Since writing requirements are part of your curriculum, be careful not to sign on for an extra paper if you know that writing is not one of your strengths.

Do you want to be in a large or small class?
There is definitely an advantage to each. In a small setting, there is one on one interaction, not only between professor and student, but also between student and student. Many individuals thrive in this environment. Bonds are created, and for those students looking for future references as well as research positions, this may be the ideal choice.

On the other hand, there are those who feel more comfortable in a crowd where they can get lost in the mix. They may not like the interaction of a small group or they may simply want the ability to skip a class now and then without being missed.

Do you need to coordinate your class schedule with a job, a clinical program, a research assistantship, or other commitments?
When a course is offered may be the ultimate deciding factor. If it is a course you must take and is only offered at 8:00 a.m., whether you are a morning person or not, you have to take it. Certain courses may only be taught in the Fall semester or only every other year, forcing you to take into account these additional considerations.

Prerequisite Intent

Every school has specific academic requirements for graduation. You alone are solely responsible for making sure that all of those preconditions are met. If you coordinate your classes judiciously, you will have the ability to create a breathable schedule while ensuring that you have completed all of the necessary criteria for being awarded your degree.

Some of the more common requirements include the following:
- total credits—You will be required to complete a certain number of credits per semester, depending on whether or not you are a full- or part-time student. There are generally a limited number of nonclassroom credit hours that you are permitted to take (*i.e.*, externships, clinical programs, independent study, etc.).
- course requirements—Depending on the school, there are various upper-class requirements that must be fulfilled in order for a student to graduate. Some schools have specific courses or programs that must be completed besides first-year mandatory classes. Keep track of which courses require you to take prerequisites. You do not want to be locked out of a necessary or desired course simply because you neglected to take the mandatory introductory class.

- residency requirements—In order to graduate from any law school, a specific amount of credit hours must be completed in-house. This is especially important to keep track of if you are a transfer student. Be sure to understand the school's policy prior to transferring.
- cumulative average status—Just as in college, there is a required minimum GPA that must be maintained in order to graduate.
- writing requirements—Each school will have writing requirements that may be fulfilled in various ways, including seminar papers, independent study papers, course papers, and/or legal writing courses.

Do not wait until your third year to determine what your requirements are for completing your program. This is something that should be investigated prior to registering for the second-year program.

chapter 8

Acclimatized Amnesty

Learning Outside of the Classroom

One of the best parts of leaving first-year law behind is the feeling that there is more to life than being buried head first in your books. There are various avenues open to students who want more than the run-of-the-mill academic experience. You will now be able to get more involved with the things that make law school a rewarding and exciting place.

Clinical Programs

Most, if not all law schools have clinical programs where students are given the opportunity to experience hands-on work with real clients. The intention is to incorporate theory with actual practice. Generally, an experienced attorney supervises the programs, and as cases come in, students are assigned to them. The atmosphere may be very much like that of a law firm. Weekly meetings or seminars might be held for the purpose of pulling together every day occurrences and coordinating schedules to meet the students' and clients' needs.

Clinical programs may differ at various schools depending on the supervising attorney's expertise. No matter what area of law your program covers, the experience will be invaluable to you in your future as an attorney, and it will stand out on your résumé. The training involved in clinical participation also brings with it the ability to sharpen the necessary skills for such tasks as interviewing clients, drafting motions and memoranda of law, negotiating with adversaries, arguing court cases, conducting depositions, mediating disputes, and many other aspects of legal practice.

Participation in a clinical program is generally limited to a chosen few due to the small number of positions available. Often, students work on cases from a location at school specifically designated for clinical programs and only leave campus occasionally for field work. However, if your school allows it, clinical participation may afford you the opportunity to intern off-campus at a local law office or government agency.

Your ability to work as an attorney prior to graduation gives you other advantages, not just the valuable experience and enhancement to your résumé, but also because of the contacts you will make that may be beneficial to you in your job search.

EXHIBIT

One attorney said that his law school had a program where students represented victims of workplace discrimination. While it was time-consuming balancing his classroom courses with his clinical participation, he said it gave him the valuable insight necessary to know that he wanted to practice in the area of employees' rights. By the time he graduated, he was fairly well-known in the legal community, giving him of an edge above the other applicants and new-comers.

The qualifications for clinical participation may vary from one school to the next, but in general, being at the top of the class is not necessarily the only way to receive an invitation to join. Unfortunately, many students shy away from applying because they think that their average grades will be a hindrance.

EXHIBIT

An attorney said that even though he applied, he never expected to be accepted into his school's clinical program. The clinical supervisor was his professor for criminal law where his GPA was a not-so-noteworthy 2.5. His main communication with the professor had come after finding a note from him in his mailbox strongly reiterating the course attendance policy. So, he was shocked when he was chosen to participate in the program representing indigent federal prisoners. When he asked the professor why he had been selected, he responded with the following reasons:

- he needed an athletic guy on the softball team;
- he liked the fact that he had a big Cadillac to drive everyone to the prison camp; and,
- he desired diversity and this guy was definitely diverse—he was at a small southern law school and he was a Jewish, Yankee, New Yorker.

The attorney said that he felt lucky to have found a professor who was not just looking for people with the best grades, but who may have had some untapped potential that they had not yet lived up to. The fact that the professor had taken a chance on him was a real turning point. He had disliked everything about law school except for the social aspects before that, and the hands-on work with clients in the clinical program made his law school experience a much more enjoyable one.

The list of clinical programs is endless. Every law school has their own distinct program to meet their particular needs. Some of those clinics include the following areas of law:

- appellate practice;
- battered women's advocates;
- child advocacy;
- constitutional rights;

- criminal justice;
- disability law;
- elder law;
- environmental law;
- housing rights;
- juvenile justice;
- legislative process;
- media law; and,
- mediation.

Acceptance into a clinical program is a wonderful way to take what you have learned in the classroom and put it to use in a real world environment. This is a transitional time for a student. It may be their first sample of life in the outside legal world. There is a big difference between book learning and hands-on experience. You can read a cook book recipe for making chocolate cake, but you will never know how well you will be able to make one until you actually prepare it yourself. Additionally, there is no better way to ascertain whether your chosen type of law is a reality for you to practice than to get into a clinical program and try it on for size.

Moot Court

This is generally the place where you begin receiving your trial court experience. The program is an excellent way to broaden your ability to perform legal analysis, writing, reasoning, researching skills, and oral advocacy skills.

There are two types of *moot court*. One is the mandatory program sometimes required during first or second year where students are given an assignment to take a position on a hypothetical case. They must write a brief and develop compelling oral arguments that are presented against an adversary before a *judge* or *panel of judges*. The panel is generally comprised of law school professors, and sometimes includes upper-level students. There is a grade given for this moot court, partially for your brief and partially for your ability to coherently argue your position.

The other moot court is the infamous voluntary competition generally entered into by aspiring litigators. These are taken quite seriously in the legal world and are valuable assets on a résumé, especially if you place well in the competition. Some schools import high-level, well-respected jurists to sit on the bench for their contests.

Moot court is a unique opportunity that challenges students to simulate actual courtroom arguments. It is also an excellent place for overcoming your fear of public speaking or to determine if you have what it takes to become a litigator. Your ability to think on your feet and argue your position clearly and cleverly is a talent that can be developed in the moot courtroom. For ambitious future litigators, there are also regional, national, and international moot court competitions.

Research Assistants

If you possess advanced research and writing skills, and you can fit it into your schedule, becoming a professor's *research assistant* can be quite advantageous. Assisting a professor with his or her research allows another avenue for honing your skills, while being guided by an established legal professional. It leaves open the possibility for acknowledgment in the professor's published work. Additionally, it may bring you some much needed extra spending money and a valuable reference for future jobs.

The research assistant generally performs such tasks as researching and recording data, cite-checking, creation of memoranda regarding research findings, and drafting of parts of the soon-to-be published articles. The position is often viewed by others as a prestigious title, if only because a law professor has recognized your abilities to be beneficial to his or her writings. However, the job may be time-consuming and may cut into your regular workload. Prior to applying, evaluate your schedule carefully to be sure that you can fit in the added work.

Law Review

The law review office is pretty much off-limits to most students who do not qualify for the prestigious title. It is a somewhat intimidating feature of law school. It is the place where articles are published after various members of the legal community, including law students, have spent many long hours writing and submitting them for review and approval. While being invited to participate on law review is generally considered to be the most exciting and sought-after activity in law school, it is important to note that there are very specific reasons why a student would want to take on the added burden of participating in this demanding activity. The most prestigious law firms interview only those students who attain law review status. The odds of getting a judicial clerkship are lessened if you do not make the cut. If you have set your sights on a starting salary of six figures or working for a well-respected jurist, this is the best way to achieve those goals.

In most law schools, law review is completely run by students. Those students are the official last word on choosing the members who participate and on which articles are extraordinary enough to reach the heights of law review stature. Schools use a variety of methods for attaining such status, including a system where a top percentage of students are automatically invited on, along with those members who win a writing competition. Also included are students whose GPA's, combined with their writing competition score, rank in the highest percentile.

Being invited onto law review is mainly accomplished by hard work and good grades. Unfortunately, the writing competition can be more about popularity.

EXHIBIT

One law student felt that it was unfair to have a writing competition since, at her school, the students on law review chose the winners. She had heard that there was favoritism because most of the people who were chosen had known each other, as well as some of the judges beforehand.

Law review status and the prestige that comes with it may be based on various factors, including how your school is ranked, how your school is viewed in the legal community, and the process by which law review invitations are determined. However your school makes the choice, learning to edit articles for law review is an invaluable experience, and prospective employers eagerly interview those who have been selected to participate. In fact, it is difficult to find a top law firm that does not advertise for those who have achieved law review status. In just about every situation, when applying for the highest paying jobs, it is a definite asset.

There is another side to the law review picture, and it is filled with those students who have no aspirations to work in a so-called cream of the crop firm, a clerkship, or a top-level corporate or government position. Some choose other avenues, such as public interest jobs, lower level government jobs, or positions with mid- to smaller-sized firms. You might wonder why anyone would opt out of those prestigious, high-paying jobs. It's very simple. Most attorneys understand that being employed at one of them will mean long hours, late nights and weekends, and no social life. Some are just not prepared to make that type of commitment and sacrifice. They may also not be interested in the kind of work offered; they might have other obligations that prevent them from accepting such a time-consuming position; or they may want to have more freedom to be with their families and friends and do not mind that their salary will not make them rich.

EXHIBIT

One young attorney said that she was so swamped with commitments that by the time she was invited to participate on law review, she decided to decline the invitation. However, she made note on her résumé that she had declined, thereby enabling her to stay in the running for top-paying jobs.

In contrast to the stereotypical view that is afloat about attorneys, some students are in law school because they have goals that reach far beyond a six-figure salary or a partnership-track position. They aspire to use their skills in a way that benefits those who are less fortunate. They do not even consider taking a position on the fast track and thus, they do not enter the law review competition.

EXHIBIT

A young attorney had applied to law school because she wanted to work in the family court system helping children. There was never a moment when she considered doing anything else. So she worked hard in school and did very well, but never felt it necessary to take that big leap to law review status.

Journals

Journals are the other student-run publications that hold prestige. Many job listings from so-called top-notch firms request that only the top ten percent with law review or journal experience apply. The major difference between law review and other law journals is that the law review journal can cover a vast array of legal subjects in each publication, while a single published law journal is filled only with articles that remain within one specific topic. If you are invited to join one of the following journals, you and your fellow journal members will always be working on articles pertinent to the journal name.

- Business Law Journal
- Constitutional Law
- Criminal Justice
- Family Law Journal
- Human Rights Journal
- Intellectual Property & Technology Journal
- International Law Journal
- Journal of Environmental Law
- Labor and Employment Law
- Law and Public Policy Journal
- Property Law
- Public Interest Law Journal

There are numerous other journals covering just about any topic of law. Depending on the school you attend, you may be invited to join using the same means by which participation onto law review is awarded.

Extracurricular Activities

Student-run organizations are rampant at law schools. The list is endless and may include such groups as the following.

- American Bar Association
- Black Law Students Association
- Business Law Society
- Environmental Law Society
- Family Law Association
- International Law Society
- Italian Law Students Association
- Jewish Law Students Association
- Minority Students Association
- Public Justice Foundation
- State Bar Association

- Student Bar Association
- Trial Advocacy Club
- Women of Law

As you can see, the choices are indicative of the diverse populations in attendance at law schools, and there are many more not listed. Any group may choose to start an organization with permission from the school. There is no limit to what you may encounter or create at the law school of your choice.

Membership in a student-run organization can be rewarding in various ways. Often, guest speakers are invited to share their expertise with the members of an association. Workshops may be held to offer students the opportunity to practice certain skills related to their particular areas of interest. Participation within the local community is also included on many club agendas. It is a good way to get to know people with common interests, and although it generally does not hold the same level of status as law review or journal experience, you will still have another glowing attribute for your résumé.

Extracurricular activities are a great way to reduce some of the everyday stresses of law school. There are also some wonderful contacts to be made through the various associations you will interact with that can be advantageous to you during your job search. Additionally, you have the opportunity to feel a strong sense of community with your classmates, as well as with those you meet through your group's outside activities.

Studying Abroad

Many law schools offer their second-year, third-year, and LL.M. students the opportunity to take classes abroad in collaboration with other law schools. Often, you can use your summer or winter breaks to earn the extra credits. The number of participants is generally limited, and the tuition (plus housing) can be quite costly. Student loans are often available to help defray costs. The schedule is coordinated to give you an accelerated program, enabling you to receive credits in a short number of weeks. The faculty is generally diverse, with some participating professors coming from foreign schools. The experience can be quite rewarding in that you will earn credits, while at the same time, have the wonderful opportunity to gain first-hand knowledge of a foreign culture.

* * * *

There you have it, an introduction to some of the choices and issues that you will face during your second year of law school; the courses to think about, the professors to choose, the activities to consider, and you have not even begun attending. This is your preamble, your introduction to the pitfalls and joys that you will encounter. Do not stop reading merely because you are not there yet. Get all of the information that you can ahead of time, so you know what to expect from the outset. Survival is possible if you are prepared for all possibilities.

The second-year task of beginning your serious job search is a huge project to be taken very seriously. The next section will be completely devoted to assisting you in preparing for your future employment as an attorney.

SECTION 5

Career Chase

I wish they would only take me as I am.
—Vincent Van Gogh

chapter 9

Finding the Right Job

Putting it All to Work

While you may take a summer position after you complete your first year of law school, your serious job search generally begins at the start of your second year. The job that you hold during your second summer of law school is often the one that you may be invited back to after graduation. Of course, this is not a rule. There are students who *are* invited back to their first-year jobs, as well as those who accept different ones after graduation. However, certain employers, especially those from the most esteemed firms, are seriously critiquing their second-year law clerks to determine who to invite back on a permanent basis. If you are planning to work at one of those *top-notch* firms, you had better not fool around while clerking there, because as cushy as the position seems—and it will appear to be somewhat soft compared to the real thing—you are being watched like a hawk for future reference.

EXHIBIT

He was already in his third year when one attorney realized how disillusioned he had been. He had always thought about becoming an attorney, mainly because he wanted to have an exciting career that would bring him a lot of money. He held summer jobs in the legal field during his first and second years.

He finally came to the conclusion that there were basically three categories of employment upon leaving law school. The first was working for large corporations or law firms anywhere from sixty to one hundred hours per week that pay out huge starting salaries; second, working for a small firm or government entity for a limited salary; and third was the mediocre-sized firm where you are caught between being rich and poor, never thinking you are earning enough, but always knowing that there is not going to be much more money where you are.

None of these choices were particularly desirable to him because he had assumed that he would leave law school and have his pick of any job he wanted. He also thought he could work forty hours a week and earn six digits right away.

Your class standing has everything to do with where you will hold your first job. That may seem reassuring to those of you who did well in college. But there is one important fact that might be eluding you. Most former top-of-the-class college students are now in fierce competition to be at the top of their law school class. The catch here is that almost everyone else in law school was also at the top of their college class. Only the top ten percent in law school generally get the highest-paying, most revered positions. Those who do soon find out that they are working for every penny they make. There is no such thing as earning a huge salary straight out of law school without giving your heart and soul to your employer. If you do obtain one of those jobs, you will work extremely long hours, get very little sleep, have virtually no social life, and little time for family. Be prepared to work under the gun and to be at your desk until all hours of the night, only to be back there bright and early the next morning. There is a steep price to pay for the prestige that you once thought was so readily available to you.

EXHIBIT

A young attorney with two small children had returned to school after divorcing her husband. She graduated law school with honors and took a job at a prestigious law firm. The money was great, but she worked so many hours that she was unable to spend any time with her sons. She was finally forced to resign. In the end, she was relieved. In her case, the pressure, stress, and inability to spend quality time with her sons was not worth the money.

However, not everyone feels that way.

EXHIBIT

A seasoned attorney recalled his first job with much pride. He worked for one of the top New York City firms and he said it felt like he never had a minute to himself. He often worked until 2:00 a.m. only to be back at his desk by 7:00 a.m. the same morning. But he loved the challenge and excitement of the job, and the money allowed him to pay off his school loans.

There is no question that sacrifices will be made both in law school and at the job of your dreams. Hopefully, you will be able to find your comfort zone and stick with it. Otherwise, you may find yourself looking in the mirror years down the line wondering what you are doing and exactly why you are doing it.

Résumé Writing— and Rewriting and Rerewriting

You are sitting in front of your computer about to type your résumé and you realize that except for your name, address, phone number, email address, and school information, the page is absolutely bare. You stop for a moment to evaluate your situation.

What can I possibly put on this resume that will make a potential employer consider hiring me? After all, I have worked as a paperboy, a waiter, a busboy, a dishwasher, a lifeguard, and a valet attendant. But, I have never worked in the legal field before.

It sounds like a real quandary, doesn't it? You have no legal experience, yet you are seeking a legal position. And you are up against some pretty stiff competition. However, do not forget that you and every other relatively new law student on the planet are in the same predicament. You are most likely viewing your situation from the wrong vantage point, thus, needlessly stressing out over your previous job titles. In reality, you should be accentuating the excellent skills you have attained from all of those nonlegal positions. An excerpt from a part of your current résumé may look like the following.

Cynthia's Roadside Lounge, Anywhere, USA
Head Bartender, January 1999 - June 2003
Responsible for hiring and training employees, opening and closing establishment, accounting for high volume receipts daily, creating and assigning employee schedules, ordering of stock.

There may be no legal experience, but it says a lot about the skills you possess.

It says somebody trusted you enough to:

- allow you to decide who works in their place of business;
- make sure the lounge opens and closes on schedule;
- take care of each day's receipts;
- understand the employees' needs and capabilities well enough to decide when they should work; and,
- keep the inventory well stocked at all times.

Prospective employers will look at those skills and translate them into the ability to supervise others, to be organized, responsible, attentive to details, to work well with others, and various other favorable attributes. Do not sell yourself short. You may have many fine qualities that a wise prospective employer will view as your true potential.

RULES FOR WRITING A RIVETING RÉSUMÉ

Your mission is to gather information. Once you have gathered all of the required materials, you will review them and delete all unnecessary items over and over until you are in possession of a refined work of art. You will then take that work of art and begin drafting your résumé. You will draft and redraft, and draft some more, until you have whittled it down to a precision document. At that point, you will then be ready to create your final masterpiece.

There are many details that are necessary for a well-balanced, winning résumé. It is not going to be as hard as you think. It is simply an autobiography, and the better it reads, the more likely you are to attract potential employers. Start by making a list of the following essential items to include on your résumé.

The names and locations of all educational institutions that you attended.
- List the dates of attendance.
- List all majors, honors, and activities for each school.
- Include anticipated date of law school graduation.
- Only include grade point averages and class ranks if you were in the top one-third of your class and only if you are listing them for both college and law school.
- Do not include your high school unless it is well-known and prestigious.

Write down every employer for whom you have worked.
You will need:
- the name of the company;
- the town and state where it was located;
- the position you held;
- your responsibilities; and,
- your dates of employment.

NOTE: Do not leave a job out simply because you did not get monetary compensation for it. The following are all respectable entries:
- volunteer work;
- internships;
- research projects; and,
- fellowships.

List every skill that went along with all of the positions and decide which are the most beneficial for prospective employers to see.
For example:
- Include that you were the first woman to hold your particular position or that you were the youngest person to be asked to join the team, etc.

Write down any special qualifications that you have that may be favorable in your job search.
For example:
- fluency in foreign or sign language or
- proficiency in various computer programs, including legal research tools such as Westlaw and LexisNexis.

If there is room, include interesting hobbies, athletic pursuits, or any other items that make you appear well-rounded.

Formatting Your Résumé

To begin, your résumé should be formatted one way if you are a recent law school graduate and another way if you have already been out in the legal world for awhile.

If you are a recent graduate, format your résumé in the following manner.
- The first items should be your name, addresses (school and home), telephone numbers, and email address, if you have one.
- Next, list your educational background, beginning with your most recently attended school.

- Enter your work history beginning with your most recent position. Describe only those responsibilities that are relevant to your job search, listing the most noteworthy first.
- Include a section with your additional information regarding other essential qualities (such as the few mentioned earlier) that might make you more desirable to a potential employer.
- Be prepared to provide a list of references.

If you are already an experienced attorney, follow the same format as that of a recent graduate, except place your work history above your educational experience.

IMPORTANT POINTS TO REMEMBER

There are certain general rules for résumé writing that you should follow.

- Be concise, well-organized, punctually accurate, brief, and do not forget to spell-check.
- Proofread your document by inspecting it word for word, because computers *do* make mistakes.
- Do not go past the preferred one page limit unless your experience is so incredible that you cannot leave something off your résumé.
- Continuously update your résumé with any pertinent information that changes your status.
    For example:
    - Make note if you have passed the bar exam and are awaiting admission.
    - If you have been admitted, be sure to include that.
    - State every jurisdiction that has admitted you.

Creative Cover Letters

Your cover letter is used in conjunction with your résumé to land you an interview. This is your opportunity to focus on specific qualities that might impress a prospective employer.

Draft a sample cover letter to use as your basic form, so you will always have a starting point from which to work. Tailoring it for each job prospect is one way to make prospective employers take notice. When writing your cover letter, it is wise to carefully research companies that interest you. Your cover letter is your first opportunity to tell a prospective employer why you are right for the job. It is your chance to stress those particular skills and attributes that separate you from other applicants. This is also your way of letting a company know that you are not sending out a mass mailing in the hopes that just anyone will respond. You want *that* job with *that* company, and it is reflected in the way that you phrase your letter.

When creating your cover letter, there are standard rules you should follow.

- Use a standard business letter format. (Find samples in your law school career services office.)
- Coordinate your paper with the one that you chose for your résumé. Do not use fancy designed or perfume-scented paper.
- Make sure the heading consists of your name, address, phone number, and email address.

NOTE: When furnishing your phone number to prospective employers, make sure there is an answering machine or voice mail to take a message if you are not there to answer and do not leave a cutesy message or funky music playing on the machine. Prospective employers look for mature, adult attorneys who are serious about their future. It is time to grow up and shed those kinky messages that make your friends laugh and leave belch noises on your machine.

- Follow the heading with the name and address of your job prospect, along with the name and position of the hiring contact.
- Insert the date.

- Find out to whom you should direct your cover letter, unless you are replying to a blind listing. (If it *is* a blind listing, it is appropriate to use "To whom it may concern.")
- Begin your letter by discussing who you are, what law school you attend, what year you are in, and the title of the position in which you are interested.
- Explain why you want this job with this particular employer and what specific attributes you possess that will be an asset to that employer.
- Highlight the parts of your résumé that directly relate to the particular position.
- Request an interview and be sure to furnish information regarding when you will be available, especially if it is an out-of-state employer.
- Stay within their preferred guidelines if a prospective employer requests a writing sample.

> **NOTE:** If they ask for a brief one, do not send your forty page paper. Send something polished (a published piece, if available) and refer to it in your cover letter. Other potential requests may be for a recent transcript or references. Only include these additional materials when expressly requested.

- Thank the person to whom you are sending your application for taking the time to consider you for the position.

Once in law school, you will have all of the resources that you need to research prospective employers, write the perfect résumés and cover letters, and know which documents should be included with them, if any. Your career services office will have more than enough information to aid you with your job search. They may even have the ability to tape a mock interview with you to demonstrate where your strengths and weaknesses lie. Utilize every available avenue to find the perfect job.

Informative Interviewing

It is 8:15 a.m., your alarm clock did not go off, and you have a 9:00 a.m. interview an hour away from home. You jump out of bed, rush into the shower, dig through your closet for some clothes, throw them on, grab a donut, and run out the door to catch a bus. The bus is late, it gets caught in traffic, you leap out six blocks away from the interview and run all the way there. You make it to the building at about 9:05 a.m., rush to the reception desk, yell out your name and hurriedly run down the hall to the interviewer's office. Somewhat disheveled, you drop your briefcase, fall into a chair, jump back up to introduce yourself, shake hands, and try to regain your natural breathing rhythm while brushing donut crumbs off your suit and dropping back down into the chair. As the inter-viewer looks you over, you offer him your excuses about the alarm clock, the bus, the traffic, and you even mention that the donut is kicking back on you. He asks a few simple questions, stands up, walks to the door, opens it, and thanks you for coming. Your inter-view is over and it is quite clear that it did not go well.

Interviewing is comparable to making a sales pitch. The inter-viewer's job is to decide who best fits the profile of an attorney who should be working in his or her firm. Your job is to demonstrate your ability to be that person. Employers are searching for people upon whom they can rely. They look for independent thinkers, attorneys who can take the ball and run with it, team players, and motivated individuals who will make their firm look good. It is your responsibility to walk into an interview in the best possible manner, laying all of your qualifications out on the table with a comfortable, professional attitude. Your first interview with a firm is your only chance to make a favorable impression. You should work as hard at preparing for it as you would for an exam.

ON-CAMPUS INTERVIEWS

In the legal arena, there are two ways to conduct interviews—one is on-campus and the other is at the office of the interviewer. Both are fairly similar, but on-campus interviews are generally shorter because there are often many students to be seen in a small amount of time. Be prepared to fit as much significant material into an interview as you can if you are meeting with a potential employer at school.

You will have the opportunity to submit your résumés and cover letters for campus-conducted interviews to either your career services office or directly to a potential employer by mail or Internet. If your materials strike an interest, you will be notified as to when and where your on-campus interview will be held. Some schools post lists of employers with the names of students who that employer chooses to interview. Sometimes, an employer will notify potential candidates directly.

On-campus interviews are sometimes seen as more stressful than those held off-campus. There is a lot of pressure put on both the interviewees and those not in the running. Often, the same students are chosen each semester for on-campus interviews by the top firms, causing added stress for those who did not get selected.

EXHIBIT

An attorney remembered all too well the day that interviews were held on-campus for a firm where she was hoping to work. Unfortunately, her name had not been on the list of students chosen for an interview with them. She saw all of the other interviewees waiting outside of the interviewer's office, well-groomed and nicely dressed in business suits. It was one of the toughest days of her law school career. She felt that it was like a double blow watching her friends, who knew of her desire to work for the firm, being interviewed while she stood on the sidelines watching.

Some students *prefer* on-campus interviews.

EXHIBIT

A third-year student referred to on-campus interviewing as *suit day*. He said that it was the day when everyone put on their best suits and strutted their stuff. He had a few on-campus interviews and he said it was great not to have to travel a long distance as he had for off-campus job prospects. He also said that it was less stressful than the off-campus interviews where you often spend hours in an uncomfortable situation wondering if you are still going to have to see others in the firm before you can escape back out into the real world and loosen your tie.

On-campus interviews are quick and are known in some circles as the *weeding out* process.

EXHIBIT

A third-year student said she hates on-campus interviews because it makes her feel as though she is on an assembly line, and there is not enough time to demonstrate her best attributes. She said that it is so quick that you leave either feeling sure that the job is yours or that you bombed. There is no in-between as there is with the off-campus interviews, where you have the opportunity to spend a significant amount of time selling yourself.

Even though some students prefer off-campus interviews, there is one major advantage of on-campus interviewing—it allows a student to continue with a fairly normal routine while awaiting interview time.

INTERVIEW ETIQUETTE

Once you are invited to interview with a firm, it means that someone has read your résumé and cover letter and they are interested in meeting with you personally to see who you really are and where you might fit in at his or her company. Someone is impressed with your credentials and wants to see the person behind the paperwork. This is when you have the opportunity to either put the icing on the cake or watch it fall before it comes out of the oven. You have an advantage in that you already have one foot in the door. A lot is riding on this meeting and you should be fully prepared to handle yourself accordingly.

The following tips are key to successful interviewing.

Research the company that is interviewing you.

Just as they are interested in finding out about you, you should also be interested in knowing all about your potential employers. Your career services office will most likely have information on all of the firms in which you are interested. Check to see if there is a firm website. Another good resource to find out information about law firms and attorneys is **www.martindale.com**.

Be prepared to answer questions.

Potential employers will ask you a wide variety of questions, including—

- Why did you decide to become an attorney?
- Why do you want to work here?
- What type of salary do you have in mind?
- What do you consider to be your strengths and weaknesses?
- What do you have to offer this company?
- Why do you think we should hire you?

NOTE: They already know what your résumé says, so be ready to add to it rather than to merely recite it.

Be prepared to ask questions.

Potential employers expect you to show an interest in their place of business by asking questions, including—

- Is there a training program?
- What is the potential for advancement?

- What are the responsibilities of an associate?
- What does the employer enjoy most about the company?
- What was it about my résumé that caught your attention?

Certain questions are better left alone until you receive a job offer—or maybe forever. Those might include—
- Do I have to work weekends and nights?
- How much time will I have for lunch?
- How many vacation and sick days will I get?
- Will I be under a lot of stress working here?
- How much are you going to pay me?
- How long before I get a raise?
- Will I get a Christmas bonus?
- Can I wait to start working here until after the summer is over?

NOTE: If an employer touches on the subject of salary with you, be prepared to offer a range that is appropriate for the position. Be careful not to undercut yourself.

Be prepared for questionable questions.
Certain issues may come up that might make you feel uncomfortable. Some of them may just be subjects that you have personal reasons for not wanting to discuss. Others may be clearly against the law for a potential employer to ask or to use as a reason for not hiring you. Attorneys should be aware that some questions are not permitted during an interview, but unfortunately, not all attorneys know the law and there are always going to be those who choose not to follow the rules. You may be faced with questions like—
- How old are you?
- Are you married?
- Do you have children?
- Are you planning to have children?

- What religion are you?
- What is your nationality?
- What race are you?

Be aware that some of those questions may be asked in much more discreet ways so as not to make you suspect anything. For example, an interviewer may ask whether or not working on certain holidays or certain days of the week is an issue for you. Clearly, this is about your religion. An interviewer may ask who resides with you. Again, a clear indication that they are trying to discern if you are single, married, or have children.

NOTE: Asking if you are of legal age for employment is totally appropriate.

Keep in mind that many inappropriate questions are asked by interviewers who are sincerely trying to make you feel more comfortable during your interview. Some do not realize the implications at all. The only way to handle this is to go with your instincts. If you feel like answering, go ahead. While it is your choice as to how you want to handle the situation, remember that some questions may be asked with a discriminatory motive. The only way you will even suspect discrimination is if you were asked certain questions and then denied the position. Of course, unless someone comes right out and tells you, you can never really be sure why you were not hired. This is one of those situations where the decision to answer a question and deciding how to handle a rejection are judgement calls on your part.

Dress properly.
Look and carry yourself as an attorney. By now, you have spent time with attorneys. You understand the dress code. You have been advised by your career counselor about the importance of

appearing as a professional. So, go with the flow and do not take it upon yourself to be different. What does that mean?

- If you have a nose ring, get rid of it for the interview.
- Do not overdo it with jewelry, and if you are in a situation or have personal issues that you do not want a perspective employer to know about yet, do not wear jewelry that reveals it (i.e., take off your wedding ring, remove the necklace with the baby charms, do not wear your *world's best grandma* necklace).
- If you have a tattoo, cover it.
- If you are a man and your hair is down to your shoulders, this is a good time to get a short and conservative cut. At the very least, tie it back.
- If you are a woman and your hair is all over the place, cut it into a neat style or tie it back.
- Whether or not you are a male or a female, wear a dark suit and conservative shoes with the proper accessories to match.
- Cologne or perfume is not a necessity. If you must use it, use it sparingly. You do not want to leave it lingering in the room long after you are gone.
- A briefcase is a good idea. If you do not have one by now, you should. But a portfolio is acceptable if that is all you have.

Prepare ahead of time.
Do not wait until the morning of your interview to gather everything you need. The night before—

- Set your alarm clock. (Leave extra time for mishaps. Remember, anything that *can* go wrong *will* go wrong!)
- Lay out your clothes and accessories.
- Put your résumé, a pad, and a pen into your briefcase.
- Determine what transportation you will take and know the schedule.

- Eat a healthy dinner.
- Review your notes about your prospective employer.
- Go to bed at a reasonable hour.

The morning of—
- Eat a healthy breakfast.
- Dress carefully and neatly.
- Take your briefcase with your résumé, a pen, and paper inside.
- Arrange your traveling time so you will arrive at least one half hour prior to the interview.
- Arrive in the area early, but do not check in until approximately five or ten minutes before your scheduled appointment.

THE INTERVIEW

This is an important day. You have labored long and hard to reach this point. Those years of school, hard work, stress, anxiety, strained relationships, financial hardships, and fears were all to get you to this very moment. As with finals, the bar exam, and most other things that have gotten you to this juncture, it is all riding on how well you perform—today. This is not meant to make you nervous. This is the wake-up call that you are getting long before you actually have to meet this moment, because, hopefully, you are not leaving for your interview when you first read this. Be prepared and be yourself. Walk into the interview feeling good about who you are, because if the law firm did not feel good about you, you would not be on your way there.

When you arrive, shake hands, introduce yourself, and make eye contact. You want to demonstrate your ability to feel comfortable in a tense situation as well as your knack for making others feel just as relaxed. You want to display masterful communication skills as well as the capacity to listen and respond accordingly.

SELLING YOURSELF WITHOUT OVERDOING IT

When discussing your attributes with a potential employer, do not overdo it. Be somewhat humble to show that you are not a know-it-all, that you are a team player, and that you are more than willing to learn to do things according to the employer's preferences. Communicate to the interviewer that you are comfortable taking direction as well as criticism, that you are a hard worker, and that you can take the initiative to work on your own.

When you get home, immediately follow-up with a letter telling your interviewer that you appreciate the time he or she spent with you. Mention a few details of your conversation so that you will stand out in the interviewer's mind. Finally, express your fervent interest in the position. Of course, this is not written in stone. There are many things that can be added depending on the interview, the type of job, your qualifications, and whether or not you really want the position or if you are merely following up to keep the door open for future possibilities.

As you can see, the entire interview process is multi-faceted. There are various stages to go through. It is important to just be comfortable with who you are and not worry about putting on an act to impress anyone. By the time you reach the door of a potential employer, you should be well-equipped with the manners and communication skills required to get through an interview. If you are not, you will not survive the job for very long. The idea is to begin preparing for this moment from the time you start thinking about what to put on your résumé. Avail yourself of every resource that is obtainable to you to plan for this day. Be confident, but not self-possessed. Follow the interview etiquette above and you will be fine.

Callbacks

If you have impressed an interviewer, you will receive what is known as a *callback*—a simple term for a second interview. This is not to be taken lightly. It is a good indication that you are in the running for the job, in the opinion of at least one person. The call-back is where you generally get to meet the rest of the gang. Hopefully, they will be as equally impressed with you as your first interviewer was. This is not the time to let your guard down. You must be as much of a professional as you were the first time around. Be careful not to replicate the first interview. You should spend some time prior to your arrival developing a new list of questions and answers. You want to appear as though you are not scripted because if the interviewers compare notes, you do not want them all noticing that you said the same things over and over.

Depending on where the interviewer's office is, callbacks can range from a free plane trip, nice hotel, meals, and town cars to a subway ride and a lot of walking. Either way, it means a fairly long day of interviews with other members of the organization and possibly future callbacks.

Callbacks are exciting and everyone waits eagerly to hear if they are chosen for a second interview. Often, it is at the second interview that a job offer may be made. If this happens, keep your feet on the ground. Remember that while you may need this job, you are interviewing the firm as much as they are interviewing you. There is something to be said for going with your gut. You should never accept a position that does not feel right, even if it was originally your *dream job*.

EXHIBIT

An attorney remembered one of her callbacks with a bit of a twinge. She said that her first interview was quite lengthy, somewhat akin to a cross-examination. The firm was medium-sized and she noticed that her interviewer, the senior partner, was a bit full of himself. She was a little nervous about a gap on her résumé because she knew that eventually, she would be asked to explain it. During the initial interview, the gap was not mentioned by her interviewer, even though he discussed her résumé quite extensively with her. He also stated that, although she did not have experience in one of the areas in which she would be expected to work, he was not concerned, saying that he would rather train her his own way then to have her come in with preconceived notions about how to do this particular task. When she left, she felt positive about her chances for the job.

She received a callback, and this time she was sent from office to office to meet all of the other attorneys, after which she was asked to wait in the conference room. A short time later, the senior partner walked in with a big smile on his face and told her that everyone loved her and that she had the job. She was thrilled until he began to discuss salary considerations. He pulled out her résumé again and started to take note of all of the items that he talked so positively about during the first interview. This time, he put a negative spin on some of them and brought up the gap.

She explained that she had taken some time off from her career because her mother had been very ill and she was needed at home for several months to help with her younger siblings until her mother recovered. Listening intently, he gazed off into the distance as though pondering how detrimental this was going to be. He looked back at her and said that, under the circumstances of the gap and the fact that she did not even have experience in one particular area, he was only willing to start her at a salary that was well below what she had originally expected.

She sat there for a moment considering her options. Here was a man who, with good reason, had been highly impressed by her credentials. She had been awarded a full scholarship to a good college and graduated in less than four years with a 4.0 GPA. She had been initiated into Phi Beta Kappa and practically every other honor society related to her degree. She performed very well in law school and had been awarded honors and scholarships for her activities and grades.

Now, after being offered the position and being told that everyone in the firm *loves her*, this man was tearing apart her impressive résumé over salary considerations. She knew what she had to do. She rose from her chair, reached out to shake his hand, thanked him for his time, and turned the job down right then and there. He was obviously flabbergasted.

His mouth dropped open and he commented, *Do you realize that you are turning down a position at one of the largest, most prestigious firms of this kind in the state? She said, Yes, I do realize that. But, to be honest, I don't feel comfortable working for a firm where I am so impressive that I am hired, but when salary considerations are discussed, I am not good enough to be offered the going rate.*

That was when he backpedaled. He offered her more money, significantly more. At that point, she had a bad taste from the experience and she declined. She said that, although it was a nice offer in the end, she has never regretted her decision to turn the job down. She felt that it was a bad start and that it would always be a situation there where she would be forced to struggle for advancement.

Have the confidence to make a decision that is right for you even if it means walking away from the job that you wanted.

Brush-Offs

It is almost certain that during your job search, you will receive your share of rejection letters. Most students do—it is just part of the process.

EXHIBIT

An attorney said that he and his friends, all successful attorneys now, received so many rejection letters that they started a *rejection* competition. They decided that whoever received the most letters would win. Additionally, if a rejection letter was especially good, the student would post it on his or her carrel, highlighting the best portions for all to see. The attorney thought he had a sure winner even though it did not come in the form of a rejection. He received a very promising acceptance letter from a fairly prestigious firm describing the various challenges that he would encounter should he decide to accept the position—as a *paralegal*.

It was an obvious error, but it brought them all a good laugh, a necessity during a very trying time. Rejection comes with the territory. Not everyone is going to like you just as you will not like every interviewer you meet. Take it for what it's worth and move on.

chapter 10

Laboring Legally

Find Your Place in the World

There are various types of employment options to choose from and you should consider each of them carefully.

Public Interest Jobs

Working in the field of public interest law is different than most other areas. The ability to have input on issues that involve human rights allows a person to touch the lives of others in a way that may forever make a difference, especially to those who otherwise might have nowhere else to turn. While most people think of public interest law as a limited area of practice, these days, the field is diverse, including issues such as civil rights, consumer rights, women's rights, children's rights, housing rights, and environmental justice. Because public interest jobs are generally non-profit, the pay is limited. But the experience is invaluable, and it will be a great stepping stone to future jobs, especially in the public sector.

The most important quality that will get your foot in the door with these employers is to have a demonstrated interest in working for the public good. It goes without saying that your specific area of interest must correspond with theirs. If they are an organization interested in working with domestic violence victims, you must have some prior experience or demonstrated interest in working in the area of women's issues, particularly if it involves victims of abuse.

Most public interest attorneys are grass-roots-types who have the unique ability in this stressful profession to be comfortable with their clients, themselves, and their work. Those who stick with this kind of work often do so because they feel they have jobs that make it easier to get out of bed every morning.

For those of you who are on the fence about public interest work due to salary considerations, it might interest you to know that there are various programs available that offer stipends, fellowships, and loan forgiveness to students who choose to work in the public arena.

Government Agencies

Government work is another public sector job that can provide an attorney with experience in almost any area of law. Different agencies will handle different areas of the law; you may be dealing with criminal defendants, environmental polluters, abused children, or Internet predators. Alternatively, you might be drafting legislation, researching charter laws, writing speeches, performing surveillance, or working in other interesting segments of the law.

Government jobs generally offer an attorney the type of consistency that many other areas of law do not provide. Working hours are usually stable, with few to no late nights or weekends, the benefits are good, there are many valuable training programs involved with employment, and there is a general sense of being part of a team.

Unfortunately, some government positions are difficult to obtain based on your political affiliations. Most of the lower level foot-in-the-door jobs are open to all of those who qualify. An appealing feature of this type of work is that it is a good starting place for an attorney who is interested in getting into the courtroom quickly without having to wade through years of research and writing as in a private sector firm.

Judicial Clerkships

A *judicial clerkship* is a wonderful way to gain experience navigating your way around the court system. The opportunity to take direction from a judge and understand the inner workings of the legal process is invaluable to your career as an attorney. Your responsibilities will be vast and may include such tasks as research, writing, and drafting memoranda and opinions, among other things. The appointment is most often a limited one, usually lasting for a one- or two-year commitment period.

The best time to begin your search for a clerkship is no later than the beginning of your second year. The deadlines for applying vary between the state and federal systems, with some states requiring that all materials be submitted as early as the spring of your second year.

A clerkship is considered to be a highly sought-after job, and only the most well-credentialed students are generally accepted. It is a position that brings with it the future opportunity to compete for the level of employment that only those in the top ten percent of the class with participation on law review or a journal are afforded.

The downside of clerking is minimal compared to the many advantages. As with government and public interest jobs, the money is not as lucrative as in the private sector. For those of you who hate hitting the books on an every day basis, there are endless hours of researching and writing. Most often, you are the anonymous force behind a judge's opinions. Do not expect to see your name in the law books or at the end of an opinion anytime soon.

A clerkship is an excellent training ground for new attorneys. What better way to gain insight into the legal profession than under the supervision of such an eminent individual as a jurist. The experience far exceeds that of newly admitted attorneys who are virtually thrown to the wolves as first-year associates in law firms. This is definitely one of the best and most appealing ways for future attorneys to make the transition from law school to legal practice.

Law Firms

Law firm sizes range from extremely large down to the solo practitioner. There are advantages to both, depending on your interests.

The larger firms generally expect more out of you, often requiring you to spend just about every waking moment fulfilling your responsibilities, and your billable hours will reflect that. They pay extremely generous salaries and offer perks not available at smaller firms. However, smaller to mid-size firms may be more family-oriented, allowing you greater leeway for a social life. The smaller firm is more likely to let the new attorney have courtroom time and hands-on experience with clients much sooner than the larger ones, where you may do a lot of grunt work at first. The focus of a smaller firm will generally be limited to fewer areas of law than the larger ones with a variety of legal departments. After spending some time in a larger firm, you generally have your pick of your next place of employment.

In-House Corporate Counsels

Corporations often hire attorneys to work in-house, to focus all of their energies on the company's business affairs. There are various differences between these jobs and the others mentioned. For one thing, working as in-house counsel often allows you the ability to work as an attorney outside of the state of your bar admission, without having to take the bar exam or waive into that state. These attorneys generally work in a legal department with several other lawyers and staff members, thus allowing them to have an extensive support system. This works well for those newly-admitted attorneys who are lucky enough to be invited to join the team.

The salaries of these jobs can be quite lucrative, depending on the status and policy of the company. The bonuses and perks can also be appealing.

EXHIBIT

One young attorney was hired as corporate counsel in an out-of-state mergers and acquisitions corporation. The business was up and coming, and the owner was quite ambitious. He offered extremely generous salaries and bonuses to his employees, and in return, had several extremely hard-working attorneys in his legal department. He also supplied apartments for those who came in from out-of-town, and all attorneys received car allowances, bonuses, and gourmet food cooked by a chef who had been hired away from a well-known restaurant.

Employees were expected to be at their desks by 7:30 a.m. and stay until after 9:00 p.m. every night. It was not unusual for them to also work at least part of the weekend. Often, attorneys rotated weekend shifts to allow out-of-towners to spend some time at home. The young attorney was not the only newly admitted lawyer there, as the general counsel wanted to have young members on his staff who could be trained to work the deals with the seasoned staff attorneys.

The pay was good, the perks were good, the experience was valuable, and the young attorney was willing to give 200% to be trained in such a lucrative environment, especially considering that she was performing the type of work that drew her into the practice of law in the first place.

Educational Endeavors

A law degree is one way to get your foot in the door for a teaching position. While rumor has it that law school professors are lawyers who could not make it in the real world, there is really no truth to that apparent myth. Often, law professors are still very active in the *real world* in one capacity or another. Some are deeply involved in their own research, a feature allowed as an aside to teaching law.

While it is a good idea to have some law practice experience under your belt prior to applying to teach at a law school, keep in mind that you must usually have some pretty hefty credentials in order to be offered one of those positions.

Pro Bono Law

Now that you have gotten past the paper work, interview process, and discussions of salary, there is an area of law that you might want to consider practicing. Law-related, nonpaying public service is a growing endeavor among law schools, private firms, and sole practitioners. Students who offer their energies to *pro bono* law are also given the opportunity to perform hands-on legal work in diverse areas.

Some law schools have instituted mandatory programs that require students to undertake *pro bono* work as part of their curriculum.

- Colombia Law School in New York requires students to perform forty hours of *pro bono* work as a condition of graduation.
- The University of Pennsylvania has a mandatory program that requires thirty-five hours of *pro bono* work.
- Valparaiso University School of Law in Indiana requires students to complete twenty hours of *pro bono* law as a requirement for graduation.

Other schools encourage students to perform free legal services by offering various incentives such as awards and/or recognition.

- Rutgers University School of Law in New Jersey hands out awards at graduation to students who involved themselves in *pro bono* work for at least three semesters.
- The University of Oregon Law School's Environmental and Natural Resources Program offers a *pro bono* certificate of completion to any student completing forty hours of *pro bono* service.

Some schools organize their own projects, while others offer students' services to local pro bono causes. This may be a student's first opportunity to touch the lives of those less fortunate, who are in desperate need of legal representation they cannot afford. It is also a wonderful way for future attorneys to see a side of life they may have never been exposed to, and to have a better understanding of the indigent population.

There are great debates going on in many state legislatures and bar associations regarding making pro bono a mandatory part of the practice of law. Some feel it is a necessary addition to the profession, while others find that they are much too busy to perform pro bono assistance and would rather donate money to the cause.

Many attorneys already provide legal assistance to the indigent and some law firms make it a regular part of their practice. For example, the following two law firms have both made commitments to donate money equivalent to at least three percent of their total billable hours to *pro bono* legal services:

- Hunton & Williams and
- Shulte, Roth & Zabel

Some firms offer incentives to employees, while many outside associations award attorneys for their participation in pro bono programs.

This may be something that you have not given much, if any, thought to while filling out your law school applications. If you have not, you might want to think about it now. As we have discussed, there are many reasons to attend law school. There is money, prestige, power, and parental pressure. If you have come to the point where you are ready to make the commitment to attend law school, then it would be wise if you considered the following. Practicing law is a profession dedicated to finding right where there is wrong, giving hope where there is none, saving those who are lost, and restoring dignity to those who are downtrodden. If you cannot understand the need to offer help to someone less fortunate, then you do not truly understand the incredible power that has been bestowed upon you as an attorney.

What better way to represent your clients than to freely defend the rights that you have taken an oath to protect? Why choose to only work for those who can compensate you financially when you have the ability to champion the poor and find a reward that pays off far more lucratively and abundantly than any amount of cash? There is no greater treasure than the relieved look in someone's eyes when you say that you will help them, even though they have no money to pay your fee. This is a wonderful reason, in and of itself, to enter into the practice of law. Please understand that nobody expects you to spend your entire life working for free. The hope is that you will do everything in your power to put some time aside to donate your legal expertise to the worthy cause of *pro bono* law.

Occupational Alternatives

Believe it or not, there are people who go through the rigors of law school and have a change of heart about their career choice, or who have absolutely no intention of becoming an attorney in the first place. Career opportunities abound for those who choose employment outside of the legal field. Nonlegal government jobs are well within your reach, along with jobs in news organizations, legal reform, consulting, academia, mediation, contract negotiations, publishing, environmental organizations, advocacy, and many other areas. Your sharpened skills will be an asset anywhere you choose to work.

To get an idea of what some well-known people have used their legal training for, check out the following list of attorneys.

- John Cleese - of Monty Python fame.
- Howard Cosell - famed sportscaster.
- John Grisham - the famous author of such books as *The Firm*, *The Pelican Brief*, *The Client*, *Runaway Jury*, *The Last Juror*, and *The King of Torts*, to mention a few.
- David E. Kelly - creator of such TV shows as *Ally McBeal*, *The Practice*, and *Boston Public*.
- Francis Scott Key - composer of the Star Spangled Banner.

- Ben Stein - probably best known for his role as the monotone teacher, Mr. Cantwell, on *The Wonder Years*.
- Senator Fred Thompson - an accomplished actor in many movies, including *Cape Fear*, *In the Line of Fire*, and *Die Hard II*, and TV's *Law and Order*.

The main point to consider when interviewing for nonlegal jobs is your ability to explain to a prospective employer why you have chosen a career outside of your field. You had better be convincing, or you may find yourself at a disadvantage if an interviewer sees you as someone who is just taking a break until something better in the field of law comes along. Be ready to sell yourself in a manner that conveys your seriousness about your nonlegal job choice.

SECTION 6

Third Year

*There are a thousand thoughts lying
within a man that he does not know till
he takes up a pen to write.*
—William Makepeace Thackeray

chapter 11

The Last Mile

Going Back to the Classroom after Graduation for One Final Test

---

You are graduating this year. By the time you have reached this juncture, you are most likely counting the days until graduation. One more degree is about to be added to your already impressive résumé. You excelled in college and you completed two years of law school. You took finals, participated in moot court, fulfilled writing requirements, got involved with activities, and you lived to tell about it. However, there are still some things that you do not know, some tasks that you have not completed, some doubts that you still have, and some questions to ask. It is not quite over yet. You are definitely in the home stretch. You are going to make it through this year, if for no other reason than because you made it through the last two. By now, you know most of the ropes, the shortcuts, the tricks, and the ways to get around the tough stuff. Hopefully, you learned it the easy way from this book rather than having to suffer through the hardships of law school life. You only need one more push to get to the finish line and this is it.

Now is the time to concentrate on more than just how you will get through tomorrow's classes, because your future is finally close enough for you to reach out and touch. You will complete any remaining academic requirements, continue with your job search (if necessary), and finally, prepare for the bar exam. It may sound overwhelming, but if you perform each task separately and efficiently, you will achieve success. Hopefully, you are aware of which courses are necessary for graduation, such as those that fulfill writing requirements and in-house credits, and you are registered for them. Third year is not the time to find out what they are. As mentioned earlier, that should have been taken care of during first-year in order to arrange your schedule accordingly. If you were careful, you were able to spread out your requirements to leave room for flexibility, leaving no room for last minute stressing out about a course that you needed, but were not able to take.

You will also want to fit in classes that are appropriate for the type of law that you hope to practice. While there is no major in law school, there are certain courses geared towards various specialties, and hopefully, you have tried to avail yourself of them while you had the opportunity. This is especially true if you already have a job waiting. Take as many courses as you can this year that relate to the type of work you will be doing. The basics of those courses will stay with you through the years as a foundation for that area of law.

You will also want to take some classes that will aid you in passing the bar exam. Information regarding the subjects covered on your specific jurisdiction's test can be obtained from various avenues, including your law school, your bar association, your state's bar examiners, and bar review course companies. This advice should not be taken lightly, because the more you prepare, the more likely you are to pass the first time around.

If you are still job hunting, you will be submitting résumés for fall and spring interviews. Third year goes by quickly, but if you are well-prepared, you will not begin to panic as graduation nears. Not everyone has a job waiting for them. Do not worry just because a few students do. All things being equal, your future will work out just as well. Likewise, not everyone is on a journal or law review or in the top ten percent of the class. Yet, somehow, most graduates do find work and survive quite nicely.

Your expectations have a lot to do with how stressful third-year is going to be for you. Be realistic about your job prospects. For example, by third year, if you have not been invited to participate on a journal or law review and you rank somewhere in the fifty percent range, do not limit yourself by only applying for jobs at the large, well-known, high-paying law firms or corporations. Unless you have some special expertise or a connection who will assist you in getting your foot in the door, you will most likely be wasting paper and time by sending résumés to those places. Setting your sights on positions in medium- to smaller-sized firms or lower level government jobs will bring you better results.

It is important to keep in mind that you should not lose hope of ever achieving financial success simply because of your law school standing. Many average law school students climb the ladder to great financial success once out in the working world. Your first job will help you to gain the expertise to move on to bigger and better things, if that is what you so desire. Depending on what type of work you choose to perform, you may never find your way into the top firms, but you may also never aspire to do so. As mentioned earlier, the trade-offs are tremendous. Whatever your career choices are, keep them realistic. Do not set yourself up for rejection and disappointment.

EXHIBIT

An attorney said that he was not the best student and felt that he would never get the prestigious job that he had always desired. He graduated at around the fifty percent mark and had not been invited to participate on any journals or law review. Upon graduation, he was offered a job as a public defender. He accepted and was so successful that the prosecutor's office lured him over to their side where he once again excelled. From there, he was offered a position at an upper level government office as a special prosecutor. After a few years, he decided to switch gears and, due to his extensive litigation experience, he was courted by a well-known law firm. He made the switch and joined their private practice. Today, he is happy and prosperous and, by the way, still only in his early thirties.

Your starting point is no indication of how far you can go in your career.

The Bar Exam

The bar exam is the most important test that you will take towards becoming an attorney. It is your ticket to practicing law. By the time you reach third-year, you will undoubtedly have been forewarned about it. You have heard stories about how draining and arduous it is and how lucky you will be to pass the first time around. The rumors are true. It is an experience like no other. Yes, you have heard that before about law school exams. Just as your entire semester grade depended on one exam, your whole career is resting on your passage of the bar.

Admittance for the bar of your chosen state requires passing more than one exam. The exams may differ from state to state, and later in this section, you will find a list of them, along with the jurisdictions that currently administer each one. With the right preparation, you *will* pass the first time around. But preparation means more than merely studying. There are other things that you will want to do to get ready for your new career. Long before graduation, you should begin making all of the necessary plans for the bar exam by taking the following suggestions.

Decide where you want to practice.

Many students attend out-of-state law schools with thoughts of practicing back at home or elsewhere. It is important to decide early on where you plan to take the bar exam, because each state has its own rules regarding fees, deadlines, and application materials.

Find out the dates of your exam.

In most states, the exam is administered in February and July of each year. However, there are exceptions; for example, Delaware does not have a February sitting.

Know which subjects your state covers.

Most jurisdictions have a specific curriculum that they use for their part of the bar exam. Find out as early as possible what it is. For example, New York state's exam covers the following subjects:

- agency;
- commercial paper;
- conflict of laws;
- corporations;
- domestic relations;
- equitable remedies;
- estate taxation;
- federal jurisdiction;
- future interests;
- mortgages;
- no-fault insurance;
- New York practice and procedure;
- New York professional responsibility;
- partnership;
- personal property;
- secured transactions;
- trusts;
- wills; and,
- workers' compensation.

Once you know which subjects are covered on your state's exam, try to take some or all of those courses in law school. It can be extremely beneficial to spend a semester studying a course that you will likely be writing about on the exam. It is important to note that most reputable bar review courses are equipped to properly prepare you to pass the exam without ever having studied the subjects during school.

Sign up for a bar review course.

There are several good bar review courses, including ones specifically aimed at the state in which you live. Your school will have information on all the programs available for you. BarBri offers several different review courses for the various exams you will need to take for every jurisdiction. Visit **www.barbri.org** for more information.

Some bar review courses are typical courses that students attend on a regular basis. Others provide individual tutoring sessions, home study courses, individual evaluation combined with personal study plans, multi-state bar exam (MBE) reviews, and essay writing instruction.

Even if you took every course in law school that will be on the bar exam, sign up for a bar review course. You will not only learn about the substance of a subject, you will also be given time-tested strategies for passing the exam.

From the time you first set foot into law school, you will be inundated with advertisements about the different bar review courses for your jurisdiction. A recommendation from someone at school will definitely be helpful and will be better suited to inform you of how to proceed in preparing for the exam than anything recommended by somebody outside of your jurisdiction.

Some bar review courses have branches located all over the United States. If you are taking the exam in a state other than where you attend school, they can still advise you on all you need to know.

Sign up as early as possible, even during first-year, to ensure locking in a price that might go up substantially by the time you are in your third year.

You may also have the opportunity to become a representative for certain bar review programs, which usually enables you to receive a generous discount for your own registration.

The Internet has a vast array of resources about the bar exam, including information regarding the different bar review courses. Simply perform a search using the keywords "bar review courses."

Take practice exams.

No matter how well you performed in law school, you will not pass the bar exam without a great deal of preparation. In spite of all of the time you spent learning your law school courses, do not think that you can study for a few nights and still pass. It is going to be a difficult test. Find as many practice exams as you can and use them—over and over.

There are many websites that offer free past bar exam questions and answers. For example—

- **http://stu.findlaw.com/thebar/samplebar.html**. This is part of the popular *Findlaw.com* site that offers free access to numerous law-related resources. Bar exam questions and answers are provided for the following jurisdictions:
    - Arkansas;
    - Delaware;
    - Maryland;
    - Minnesota; and,
    - Texas.
- **http://stu.findlaw.com/thebar/results/index.html**. Also part of the *Findlaw.com* website, this site offers a wealth of bar exam information for fifty-one jurisdictions, including past exam questions and answers.

There are also several sites that offer past bar exam questions and answers for sale.

- **www.ncbex.org/pub.htm**. This is the site for the National Conference of Bar Examiners. Offered are past

Multistate Bar Exams, Multistate Professional Responsibility Exams, Multistate Essay Exams, and Multistate Performance Tests (all to be discussed later).

- **http://law.slu.edu/academic_support/sample_exams.html** This is Saint Louis University School of Law's link to past exams from approximately fifty jurisdictions, including patent bar exams.

For a more complete list of websites, a quick keyword search on any Internet browsers for "bar exam questions and answers" pulls up a multitude of links for past exams in every jurisdiction.

Outside the Test

The exam may last up to three days, depending on your jurisdiction. No matter how long it is, it will take a toll. The months that follow waiting for the results will also weigh heavily on you. For the time being, focus on the present and on how to get through the exam without losing your sanity.

Aside from the previous suggestions, preparation should also include creating a checklist of things that will serve to make exam time somewhat easier to tolerate.

Include the following on your list.

Secure lodging.

If you live a long distance from the test center, consider getting a hotel room for the night before the exam. There are many horror stories about applicants getting stuck in traffic or having their car break down on the morning of the exam. There is no need to put yourself through the added stress of having to make your way there if you can stay close enough to walk to the center on the morning of the exam. Hotels generally have special rates for bar applicants.

Decide what items to bring.

At the exam site, you will have to produce your identification. There is a good reason for this. People have been caught attempting to take the exam for others. You must be able to prove who you are.

There may be other materials necessary for your admission to the exam. Find out in advance what they are and pack them the night before.

There are limitations to what you are allowed to carry into the test center with you. For example, the New York State Board of Law Examiners requires that applicants carry any allowable items in a clear plastic bag, no larger than one gallon size, and it can only contain the following items:

- admission ticket;
- government issued photo ID;
- wallet;
- quiet snack/lunch;
- hygiene products;
- earplugs;
- pens, #2 pencils, erasers, highlighters;
- beverage in plastic container or juice box, 20 oz. max.;
- medications; and,
- tissues.

Prohibited items include:

- handbags, purses, backpacks, briefcases, tote bags, luggage;
- notes, books, bar review or other study materials;
- electronic devices, cell phones, calculators, pagers, programmable watches, clocks, cameras, radios, recording devices, hand-held computers, any type of personal digital assistant, wireless email devices;
- headphones or headsets; or,
- weapons.

These are strict rules that must be followed. Do not deviate from them or you will end up losing your property on the day of the exam. This will only make your stress level higher than necessary.

Since you can bring very few items, be selective. Many people feel that the most important article to have is a watch to keep track of time. Remember to leave anything you do not consider a necessity at home or in your hotel room.

If, for some reason, you have special circumstances that require you to carry in a forbidden item, be sure to request permission prior to exam day.

Several jurisdictions now allow applicants to use their own personal laptops to take the exam. There is an extra fee for utilizing the specialized technology that essentially prevents test-takers from accessing any other information on their laptops during the exam. Additionally, some test sites limit the amount of students allowed to use a laptop for the exam. You must arrange to use your laptop ahead of time.

Request special accommodations in advance.

If you require special accommodations, such as a large print exam, elevator access to the test area, extra time, or any other type of assistance due to a mental or physical disability, make sure to request them in advance. You will be required to furnish written documentation of your need, so be sure to know what to do in advance and what the deadlines are for your request.

Relax and enjoy yourself the night before the exam.

There is a lot to be said for clearing your head the night before an exam. You do not want to be a victim of overkill. Too often, students are so crazed, they spend every waking moment right up to exam time studying. This is a bad idea. You are already frazzled. You have spent approximately twenty years in school. You have just endured three of the most grueling of those years in law school. Hopefully, you took a bar review course immediately after graduation. To put it plainly, you have prepared enough. If you still need to study the night before the exam, you are in big trouble. You will clog your head needlessly, because if you do not know enough to pass by now, one more night will not help.

Dress comfortably.

You will be sitting in an uncomfortable chair all day long for as long as three days. Wear anything that gives you the flexibility to move around. Make sure to dress for all conditions—cold and warm. You never know if the air conditioning will be somewhat akin to the law library at midnight or if the heat will be putting you to sleep. Dress lightly and bring a sweater, sweatshirt or coat, whatever the season demands, and prepare for the exam room to be either too cold or too hot.

Certain jurisdictions actually have specific dress codes you must follow. For example, if you are in Kentucky or Virginia, be prepared to wear a suit during the entire exam.

Prepare to stay focused.

There will be many distractions on the day of the exam. The guy next to you might be tapping his pencil. The woman in front of you might be shifting around in her seat. The person behind you might have a cold and sneeze and cough for hours. You could be in the seat right by an exit for the bathrooms. Every little thing may drive you crazy on that day. By now, you have a good idea about how well you can tune others out during exams. Be prepared with earplugs or whatever you need to focus your attention where it needs to be—on your exam.

EXHIBIT

A young law graduate who had recently taken the bar exam said that the person behind him kept smacking his lips on a snack

> throughout the entire day. Not wanting to make an issue of it, he tried as hard as he could to ignore the noise. Finally, out of desperation, he went into the bathroom, rolled up tiny pieces of toilet paper and stuffed them into his ears. It was not quite as good as ear plugs, but it did muffle the sound.

Even when you have been able to focus on exams in the past, do not underestimate the power of stress at this all-important time to make every little noise seem amplified beyond normal tolerance levels.

Other Stressful Stuff

As mentioned previously, there are various exams that are required for admittance to the bar depending upon your jurisdiction. Below is a list of some of those exams along with a few small details about each of them.

MULTISTATE BAR EXAM (MBE)

The Multistate Bar Exam (MBE) is a six-hour exam consisting of two hundred multiple-choice questions covering Constitutional Law, Contracts, Criminal Law and Procedure, Evidence, Real Property, and Torts. The test is divided in half, with a three-hour session in the morning and a three hour session in the afternoon. As of this writing, it is being administered twice a year in fifty-three jurisdictions, not including Puerto Rico, Washington, and Louisiana.

MULTISTATE PROFESSIONAL RESPONSIBILITY EXAM (MPRE)

Currently, not every state requires the Multistate Professional Responsibility Exam (MPRE) for admission to the bar. However, fifty-two jurisdictions do require it, not including Maryland, Puerto Rico, Washington, and Wisconsin. It is a two-hour and five minute exam administered three times a year in March, August, and November. It consists of fifty multiple-choice questions aimed at the laws governing the conduct of attorneys. Additionally, ten more questions are included that ask for the examinee's reactions to testing conditions.

Multistate Essay Exam (MEE)

The Multistate Essay Exam (MEE), administered in February and July of each year, is currently used in seventeen jurisdictions, including Alabama, Arkansas, District of Colombia, Guam, Hawaii, Idaho, Illinois, Kansas, Kentucky, Mississippi, Missouri, Nebraska, North Dakota, Northern Mariana Islands, South Dakota, Utah, and West Virginia. It is a three-hour exam, consisting of six essay questions. It tests the applicant's ability to:

- identify the legal issues in hypothetical questions;
- distinguish between relevant and nonrelevant information;
- analyze relevant issues; and,
- show an understanding of the legal principles relevant to the likely solution of the issues raised by the facts.

Multistate Performance Test (MPT)

The Multistate Performance Test (MPT) is administered in thirty-one jurisdictions, including Alabama, Alaska, Arkansas, Colorado, Delaware, District of Colombia, Georgia, Guam, Hawaii, Idaho, Illinois, Indiana, Iowa, Maine, Minnesota, Mississippi, Missouri, Nevada, New Jersey, New Mexico, New York, North Dakota, Northern Mariana Islands, Ohio, Oregon, Rhode Island, South Dakota, Texas, Utah, Vermont, and West Virginia.

The exam, offered in February and July of each year, consists of three, ninety-minute skills questions for the purpose of testing the applicant's ability to use fundamental lawyering skills in realistic situations. The MPT requires applicants to:

- determine which facts are relevant;
- analyze statutory, case, and administrative materials for relevant legal principles;
- resolve a problem by applying the relevant laws to the facts;

- identify and resolve ethical dilemmas, when present;
- demonstrate the ability to communicate effectively in writing; and,
- complete a lawyering task within time limits.

For more information on the exams, go to **www.ncbex.org/tests/ mpre/mpre.htm**.

Soothing Thoughts

A few more things bear mentioning about bar exam day.

Missing a point does not mean failure.

Just because you missed one or two points on an essay, that does not mean failure. No matter which jurisdiction you take it in, it is a long, complicated exam. There is always going to be room for error. You do not have to achieve a perfect score. Even if you miss an element of a crime or a policy issue, that does not mean that the whole essay is wrong. There are a lot of different methods for awarding points, so never take it for granted that you failed after realizing that you may have missed an issue. If you feel rushed and do not have enough time to finish an essay—

- list the issues;
- list the elements;
- list the rule;
- attempt a brief analysis; and,
- come to a conclusion.

If you have less time than what it takes to do the above—

- list the elements (that, in and of itself, will gain you some points).

The key is to keep going. No matter what the problem is, even if you are sure that you have already blown the exam, finish it and do your best.

Do not discuss the exam.

On the evening after your first exam day, when you are sitting with a group of friends having dinner, do not discuss the exam. I repeat, DO NOT DISCUSS THE EXAM! There is no benefit in talking to others about the questions. Everyone has a difference of opinion about what the right answers are. Avoid putting yourself in the position of stressing out over a fellow test-taker's remarks about how he or she handled an essay. You might have been the one who got it right.

Nonfatal Failure

It bears mentioning that people do fail the bar exam and it is not always because they had not worked hard to prepare themselves. Sometimes, other factors intervene that make it difficult to perform adequately. There are those who are not able to deal with the stress. There are others who have not grasped the art of analysis or the skills necessary to write a passing essay. It is not uncommon to hear about someone who, after months of strenuous preparation, woke up under the weather and took the test with a fever or bad cold only to fail. A family emergency, a car accident, a stalled car or flat tire the morning of the exam, a faulty alarm clock, a stomach virus, a sick child, a snow storm, a bad headache, and many other things may happen on your all-important day. The only advice for those moments is to roll with the punches. Remember, the test is given more than once a year. People who fail generally do pass the second time around. Most employers allow for one or two failures before letting you go. It is not the end of the world if you fail, and in the long scheme of life, your failed exam will be a thing of the past in a short time.

The only person who will suffer great disappointment from your failure is you. Do with that what you will, but do not carry it with you like an albatross. Move on and pass the next time around.

The exam is stressful, but as difficult as it may be, the fact is that in New York State alone, of the 9,407 applicants examined on July

29–30, 2003, 6,532 passed. Of the 7,761 applicants who were taking the exam for the first time, 6,024 passed. The odds are in your favor. The key is preparation.

The much-publicized John F. Kennedy, Jr.'s two bar exam failures should leave you with these two important thoughts—

1. failing the bar exam does not ruin your career and
   - All attorneys are aware that many smart people do not fare well on exams.
2. only famous people have their failures publicized.
   - You do not have to list your exam failures on your résumé.
   - Unless you have a job where your employer is aware that you have taken the exam, nobody needs to know how many times you have taken it.

If you know that you are not a strong test taker, you should compensate for it on an exam of this level of importance by going the extra mile with your preparation. It is usually not a matter of test-taking abilities that causes people to fail. Rather, it is their lack of seriousness about how much preparation is required. There are those people who excelled in law school and feel that they do not have to work as hard to pass the bar because they think they have all they need. However, bar review courses hold a wealth of information regarding what subjects are covered, what strategies to use for tackling the multiple choice part, essay-writing tips, and more. You are really short-changing yourself if you choose not to take one.

Bar None

Believe it or not, there are law students who never take the bar exam or have failed and choose not to try again. Of course, in almost every state, you cannot practice law without passing it, but sometimes, that is the plan. If the career path that you have decided to embark upon does not warrant a license to practice law, then there is no reason to go through the stress of preparing and sitting for the bar. As you have seen in this book, there are other careers besides law from which to choose.

What Next?

You have gotten over the last big hurdle. The bar exam is now behind you and the waiting begins. Whether or not you have a job lined up, take some time to clear your head. If possible, arrange to have at least one month off prior to beginning your law career. Many employers allow for some time after the bar exam for you to regroup. They are not any more anxious to have a stressed out new attorney than you are to be one. Do something fun. Plan a vacation, take a road trip, veg out on the beach, get some much-needed sleep, rent some funny movies, visit old friends, or spend quality time with your family. In other words, take back your life!

The bar exam results generally take a number of months to post. It is a time when most of you who have jobs will prepare to begin working and those of you who do not will continue in search of one. You will have been informed as to how long it will take to receive your particular exam results. You must somehow find a way to put the test in the back of your mind for awhile and focus on other things. When the time draws near, you will undoubtedly begin to get anxious. Do not let your fear of failure keep you from moving forward. Remember, your future employers are also attorneys and they know very well the difficulties of taking the bar exam. Many of the brightest students do not pass the first time around. Good test takers do not necessarily make good attorneys and bad test takers do not make bad attorneys.

The exam is pretty much just another stressful event in your life that is part of your initiation into the world of law. It is no better an indicator of what kind of attorney you will be than the LSAT is of how well you will perform as a law student. Do not forget how much you have already survived. If you have reached this juncture, you are pretty incredible! Be proud of yourself and keep your chin up, no matter how you fare on the exam!

SECTION 7

After School

*The credit belongs to the man who is actually in the arena,
whose face is marred by dust and sweat and blood; who
strives valiantly; who errs and comes short again and
again, who knows the great enthusiasms, the great devo-
tions, and spends himself in a worthy cause; who at best,
knows the triumph of high achievement; and who, at the
worst, if he fails, at least fails while daring greatly, so that
his place shall never be with those cold and timid souls who
know neither victory nor defeat.*
—Theodore Roosevelt, "Citizen in a Republic,"April 23, 1910.

chapter 12

What You Really Learn in Law School

Skills You can Hang Your Shingle On

Law school is not just about lawyering. It is about artful arguing, moderate mediating, rationale reasoning, and thoughtful thinking. It is a place where skills are sharpened like tools of the trade and minds are molded into flexible, yet factual, matter. It is where you let go of your inner child and become a serious grown-up. You will no longer be able to focus on your creative side, because that part of you is beyond the realm of mere fact. You will learn to take criticism, deal with sarcasm and humiliation, and be reprimanded for not saying exactly what someone else wants to hear *when* they want to hear it. Mind reading will become one of your most desired character traits. You will be trained to write an essay or a paper—a different way for each professor. You will learn how to argue, win, mediate, mitigate, advance, and retreat. It is a survival game. Those who have the most endurance will triumph. The goal is not just about walking out as a finely tuned attorney. You will become more analytical, more reasoned, and more even-sided. You will have gained insight into worlds previously beyond your realm, and you will never again be the same person as when you first entered the hallowed halls of law school.

The skills that you present as an attorney are useful tools that will work for you in any profession. You are not tied to the law merely because you have obtained a degree. You will be a good negotiator, a meaningful advocate, and a thoughtful colleague wherever you go and in whatever profession you decide to join. No matter how you choose to utilize your law degree, the skills that you have honed will help you accomplish your goals.

Objective Thinking:
The Key to being a Competent Attorney

When you arrive at law school, you must be prepared to sharpen the skills that will become your survival tools. However, these particular skills are not character traits that you will acquire while in school. They are the gifts that you have carried through life, hoping to one day refine and utilize to the point where you can achieve the great things you so desire. In law school, you will struggle through open debates, grilling question and answer sessions, the boring briefing of cases, and the ritual of oral presentations. You will read old, stuffy decisions of jurists long gone and the opinions leading up to them. You will learn to develop and formulate arguments, and hopefully have the chance to use the knowledge that you have gained to put your skills into practice before you graduate. You will watch other attorneys as you move through your three year stint, hoping to gain insight into how they proceed with their cases. You will try your best to remember their strategies while also taking heed of their follies.

Nobody can teach you how to be a good lawyer. In law school, you learn caselaw and the principles and rules that make up the opinions in those cases. However, your most useful asset is not what you learn substantively. As in college, the subject matter of courses can be learned by anyone. The difference here is that you must understand how to transform that subject matter into well-developed policy analysis, thought-provoking strategies, and possibly, finely-tuned legal doctrine. Your inherent skills will be honed to assist you in performing these tasks.

There are other sharpened skills that you will hopefully carry away with you. Those include the ability to separate fact from fiction, to recognize mitigating circumstances, to look beyond what you once perceived as merely right and wrong, and to understand that no matter how terrible the situation, every person deserves a defense. This type of thinking is not only appropriate for attorneys, it is also useful for many other professionals and people from all walks of life.

EXHIBIT

An attorney stated that she had not been happy practicing law and decided to go back into her previous career of sales. She said that now, she is much more successful at her former profession, but does not regret putting herself into debt by going to law school. She credited her training as an attorney with enhancing her power of reasoning and persuasion, and said that those attributes had definitely made the difference for her this time around in her sales career.

There is no question that you cannot leave law school the same as when you first arrived. If you do fairly well, it is because you have caught on to the lingo, the way of life, and the rules of the profession, as well as the need to rearrange your thought processes. You will become more well-rounded. It is a way of thinking that often makes you sit back and wonder how you got along in your life with such a closed mind. Prior to law school, you may have been more apt to stay within the lines than to read between them. You may have been afraid to step outside of the box.

Now, you jump back and forth without a thought. You realize the need to examine every detail, not just those that you normally would have noticed before law school. In the legal world, you must be able to perceive and understand all sides of an issue. You must also be comfortable recognizing that there actually *are* two or more sides to an issue. You may have previously been led to believe that things are either right or wrong, black or white. You will now be introduced to the concept of the *gray area*, where things can get quite fuzzy. This is the place where your analytical and reasoning skills are the most helpful.

For example, you have always viewed people's actions as either good or bad. You think that anyone who commits a crime should be punished. But each case has its own set of unique circumstances, and it is these circumstances that make the difference between cases. You hear all the time about two seemingly exact situations where one person gets acquitted and the other one goes to jail. You discuss it with your friends and come up with all sorts of explanations. *He was rich, so he could afford an expensive attorney. His lawyer must have been a friend of the judge's. He was white.* You never really think about the *mitigating* circumstances behind the court's decision. They are the details that make the *exact same cases* different. They are the factors that can determine the difference between jail and acquittal. If you really give this some thought, you will realize that you are lucky to have a system that weighs all of the facts before imposing a punishment, because you might find yourself or a loved one on the hot seat some day.

Of course, there are real, hardcore criminals out there. They may be people who have decided that the world owes them everything they want. Or, they may have no concept of the fact that they are committing a crime. Maybe they were raised in an environment where there were no boundaries, no directions as to what is right or wrong, where a bitter parent instilled in them that everyone is out to get them and that they have to take what they can or lose out.

Everyone has something underlying their actions and everyone deserves to be heard and defended, no matter what the reason is for their actions. The people who you perceive as just plain bad may be people who have merely gone astray and need some help getting back on track. They may be mentally ill and need representation to ensure that they get the proper help they so desperately need. Even if they are just so far gone that they should not be running loose in the world, they deserve to have a fair trial. You may find yourself across the table from a rapist, a child molester, a burglar, a drug dealer, or a murderer. It might be a woman who killed her husband after he beat her.

The situation may not even be criminal. You might be at a firm that handles environmental issues and your boss may be telling you to continue with a contract for property even though you know that there is a serious pollution hazard involved. That is not to say that you are being told to do something illegal. There are just times when you know something, but due to the position that you are in, it is not your responsibility to divulge certain information. It will be the moment of truth for you. You will either have to do what you are sworn to do or what your boss is directing you to do. As time passes, and you gain more authority at your job, you may be in a position to choose the cases that make you more comfortable. Either way, if you have been trained well, you will find yourself more open-minded about who you will defend or what position you will take. You will be more accepting of the fact that there are mitigating circumstances that must be seriously considered in all cases.

Objectivity should also help you recognize the need to turn down cases when you do not feel there is merit to a claim. There will be other times when you will send them away because you do not believe that you can prevail. Then, there will be those instances when you turn a case down because you cannot, in good conscience, represent the person, for whatever reason. You may also find yourself declining to represent someone because you feel that, even though there was harm, it is so minor that the case would merely amount to nothing more than revenge. You may find yourself struggling with a decision to take a case that you know is not likely to prevail, but you feel strongly enough about the issue to put your energies into defending anyway.

Hopefully, you will give great thought to which cases to take and not let your decision rest merely on financial gain. There are cases that you will know to be losers in reality, but, due to a lack of evidence, you may actually win. If you know that your client does not deserve to be the winner, you may decide to follow your conscience and let the case go. However, it is important that you keep an open mind and listen to the feelings and thoughts of your clients before determining whether or not you consider it appropriate to represent them.

As you can see, there is so much more to using your brain than following the well-meaning guidance of those who have often lectured you about the ways of the world. You now know that there is something to be said for extenuating circumstances and that not everything is the way it seems. In essence, you have been reprogrammed. You may graduate with the brief thought that you would like to go back to the way you viewed things before law school. There was an innocence back then, a naiveté that you were comfortable with because you did not have to think as much. Your mind was tuned in to only the limited notions of black and white, right and wrong. You were just another person. You did not have to watch your words out of fear that you would be held to a higher standard than most others. People did not stop what they were doing to hear what you had to say about a subject. Now, your advice is taken seriously, very seriously.

Everybody thinks you know everything about the law. However, you do not, and explaining that is not as easy as it seems. So, you try to ease your way around it. You make excuses and you backpedal. You try to do the right thing and people do not always understand that you are just a human being with a little more knowledge than lay people about legal issues. One thing you do have that stands out above the average Joe is your newly developed ability to envision things that are not obvious to the untrained mind. It is called *total objectivity*.

Speaking like a Lawyer

Though the thought of having to defend a position in law school may be somewhat intimidating at first, you should realize that this is a skill you have used your entire life. As a child, you may have negotiated for that extra cookie or to stay up late on a school night. Maybe you talked your way out of being punished or into using the family car. You might have even weaseled your way into first class on a flight. Those raw skills have carried you through many *deals* that you have made, and now, in law school, you will be given the opportunity to cultivate and perfect the fine art of arguing your position. There will be many chances to state your case and hear your opponent's viewpoint. It may come in an assignment, a moot court argument, on an exam, during a classroom debate, or in an informal study group.

The one thing that is certain, there will come a time when you will be faced with having to defend a position, one that may even be contrary to your own beliefs. Your feelings on the matter will not be an issue. You will look at the case you are handed and you will do whatever is necessary to learn how to view both sides of the issue, how to formulate an argument, and how to come to a conclusion, while sticking to the facts and backing up your position with firm evidence. You will recognize that your own ability to come across as secure in your argument can actually make your opponent question his or her own posture on a subject. You will understand that even when you are caught off-guard, you will be able to find a way to pull yourself back to a solid stance. You will see that losing is nothing more than not presenting the best argument. Arguing a case is truly a duel of words.

Looking at Life in Real Terms

Attorneys do not know everything about every facet of law. As a matter of fact, they do not really even know close to everything. They may know a lot about one specialized area, if they have been practicing it for several years. What they recall about all other areas is most likely from remnants of a law school lecture that was deeply embedded in their brains. Thus, when you are cornered somewhere by a well-meaning acquaintance seeking legal advice outside your area of expertise, and you *will* be, do not hesitate to answer that you do not practice that type of law and tell them to retain an attorney who does. Then, go on your merry way without a care in the world. Never underestimate the power of simply saying that you do not know, even if it is about something that is related to your field of practice. You will have to work for years before you can answer every question about your own specialty without having to check into it first.

Walking the Line

I am going to let you in on something that permeates the legal world, but that attorneys do not share with those outside of the profession and often, not even with their colleagues. We are reluctant to let it be known that there are those of us who are as disenchanted with our careers. We are in a different situation than others in different professions because we have to live by a code. We have a duty to be ethical, to uphold justice, to protect and defend, and to represent all who are in need of our advocacy. Most of us walk a fine line. It is a line of conscience. Some cross it, some do not. In law, the line is often fuzzy. Most have learned through experience that crossing it is the best way to survive the profession. However, going against your own beliefs can be extremely damaging if you have not yet reached the point where you are able to separate your emotions from your cases.

Attorneys are expected to be objective, yet caring; emotionless, yet passionate; honest, yet crafty. Many earn far less than those who have not even been awarded college degrees. We are advised to treat our clients in a professional manner, to be their shoulder, their counselor, their protector, and their defender. We are to be tireless champions of good, winners against evil, warriors of right. We are expected to be on call for our clients and to expand our representation to include all of their concerns, rather than just the one that brought them to us. We are not allowed to leave our work at the office or in the courtroom. We must, at times, lie awake at night pondering a solution for their problems. As officers of the court, we are held to a standard higher than most. We must be completely ethical without error, without fault, without thoughtlessness. Those are big shoes to fill. We are capable of filling them on an intellectual level, but filling them on an emotional one is not as easily done.

There seems to be a void and it appears to begin at the source— law school. From the moment you arrive, during your intermittent periods of relief from anxiety, you are virtually inundated with the axiom that you are special, so special, in fact, that you do not need to have any type of reinforcement or reassurance. You are expected to be strong, self-assured, and capable of handling everyone and everything. Yet, strangely enough, this is never discussed in law school. There are no courses on bedside manner or handling a difficult client. There is no instruction regarding how to survive losing a case or watching a client being taken away in handcuffs. There is no seminar teaching us how to balance our professional lives with our personal lives or how to cope with the everyday stresses that fill our calendars. We are indoctrinated and shipped off to war with only the barest of battlefield training. We go out like champions, only to return home like rag dolls. There is no better way to describe the disappointment and frustration that many attorneys have with their profession. If we slip and do something "wrong," we are frowned upon as though we are not capable of being human. We are not allowed to make mistakes like everyone else, because our mistakes will cost us our licenses. Our burden is a heavy one.

The lawyer who stays on the straight and narrow, never straying, never telling a little white lie, never advising a client incorrectly, whether unintentionally or deliberately, never withholding information that could change the outcome of a case, never saying or doing whatever it takes to beat an adversary, never accepting a case just for the money (even if it goes against the grain), will eventually find themselves very much alone in the profession. Something appears to take hold of many of us and it leads us down a path that is sometimes dark and lonely. We hopefully enter the profession of law with the best of intentions, the highest of values, the deepest concern for our fellow man, and we soon get stuck in the muck and mire of compromise, lack of sleep, lack of family life, and lack of who we once were. We change and the change is noticeable by all around us. It comes with a wrinkled brow, a downward frown, tired eyes, distant stares, mumbled responses, and hopeless thoughts.

We were once like children who felt excited about our new endeavor. We worked hard, never noticing the gradual transformation into the worn out souls that some of us had become, because we were unprepared and uneducated about what we were going to experience as attorneys. Our creativity and sense of joy and excitement have all been tamed. We have raised the bar on ourselves, not because we wanted to, but because there was no choice. We are now factual beings, filled with accuracies and literal objectiveness. We claim that our quest is for justice, yet, our sense of righteousness is often only for our own clients, right or wrong, innocent or guilty. We start to look at them as our bread and butter. In the beginning, a client would call and we would be concerned about his or her well-being. Now, we start to think about our own state of existence.

EXHIBIT

An attorney who has been in practice for many years said that early in his career, he was a caring person. He referred clients to other attorneys when necessary and advised them as to how to handle some things on their own, when feasible. But, as time passed, his thinking changed. He became more cynical. He had gone into private practice and he started looking at cases in terms of the money; the more clients he had, the more financial gain he would incur. He found that when people called him inferring that they might be in trouble, he secretly hoped that they were, rather than thinking about their well-being as he used to. That way, he could charge them a large fee. In turn, they would refer him to others and his name would be passed around and he would make even more money. As he discussed this, he said that it was sad, because he felt as though he was living up to the

> public's perception of attorneys, that they feed off of other's misery. But, he added, it's ironic, people see us as sharks and ambulance chasers, yet, when they find themselves in a jam, they run right to us and beg us to crush their opponent.

Though the change is gradual and often unnoticed by us, years later, we may look back and find a trail of dissatisfaction in our path. We want to change the impression that the public has of us, but the truth is that one lawyer has to win and the other has to lose. The losing party and all of his friends and family hates the winning lawyer and that hate festers and spreads like a virus. Everyone feels as though they should win. Even *we* believe that we should win.

We learn too soon that our idealism, combined with our desire to achieve success, is like a poison that infiltrates our reasoning ability and leaves us vulnerable. We either end up in a compromise or we end up torn to shreds. Those of us who are lucky enough not to have to bend are few and far in between. We are often the ones who can lift our heads from the pillow each day with a smile. We have remained ourselves somehow, to be true to our original goals and loyal to our own ideals.

Comfort Zone

At one time or another, an attorney questions his or her reason for practicing the type of law that he or she has chosen. Those who are true to themselves will leave an uncomfortable situation and move on to something more palatable. However, not everyone has the means, the strength, or the courage to do that. Once you are in a solid job situation with salary and benefits, a desk with pictures of your family, and diplomas on the wall, it is hard to pick up and move on. There are many fears regarding the risks of change for most people, not just attorneys. For attorneys, especially ones with tens of thousands of dollars in school loans to pay back, change is very frightening, so some get stuck.

Many a law student entered school with one direction in mind, only to shift gears along the way. Whether it was due to a change of heart or having the wrong credentials, they went into areas of law that were not what they had intended when they applied to school. Some found their way back to their original paths and others felt that they had invested too much time in one direction to start over again in another area.

Law students are rarely, if ever, informed that there are certain areas of law that are extremely difficult to get their foot in the door of straight out of law school. Some students enter school knowing the type of law they want to practice and take as many courses in a particular area as they can, only to find that nobody wants to hire a *wet behind the ears* attorney. If there is a specific area that you have in mind, investigate your possibilities for employment either prior to or soon after entering law school. Try to determine if the area is one that requires that you be at the top of your class or have law review or journal status. If so, that is what you have to strive to achieve.

There seems to be a catch-22 regarding experience in certain fields of law. While job hunting, you will find that there are listings that make very little sense. The ad may appear to be aimed at you. However, after closer inspection, it is obvious that there is no real rhyme or reason for its placement where you found it. For example, the following was a recent listing.

Commercial litigation firm seeks recent law graduate for associate position. Must be able to handle all aspects of litigation. Duties include depositions, court appearances, and extensive legal research and writing. Successful candidate will be willing to work some evenings and weekends. Prior law firm experience, including at least 4 years of solid, commercial litigation experience, preferred. Must have knowledge of Lexis. Salary commensurate with experience.

This listing was posted on a site in the area designated for attorneys with "0 years experience." The ad itself states that the firm is seeking a recent graduate. Yet, a closer look reveals that they prefer someone with at least four years of litigation experience. How can they expect a recent law grad to already have four years of commercial litigation experience? This is frustrating to the new attorney who is ready and willing to work hard. As you will see, certain areas of law are off limits to the new attorney. When you take a job in another area, thinking that you will gain enough experience to change over to the field of your choice, keep in mind that you may be sealing your fate. If you take a criminal law position because you cannot get into an environmental firm right out of school, you will be gaining experience in criminal law. Why would an environmental firm take you two years down the line with all of your criminal law experience? Sometimes the best chance that you have is if you are a seasoned litigator. Experienced and successful litigators are a commodity. You can always learn a new area of law, but having litigation experience under your belt is extremely desirable. If environmental litigation is your preference, litigating in another area is not ill-advised. Otherwise, switching gears to try another type of law will be very much like starting from scratch.

As you can see, making the choice about what type of law you will practice is not as simple as it seems. It may be a decision that your entire career rests upon. Investigate many areas of law while you are still in school. Take different jobs during your summers to get a taste of the various legal fields. Apply for a clinical program or an internship. If you are interested in a job that has no openings, offer to volunteer your services for a few hours a week just to see how you like it. There are many legal practitioners who would love to have a free law clerk around for awhile.

EXHIBIT

An attorney working in the district attorney's office said that during law school, she was interested in clerking in a government agency's domestic violence division. The job was one where employees had to go through a long application process, and then wait to be chosen from a list of several applicants. She was only interested in working there during the summer of her second year. So, she applied for a fellowship at school that offered a stipend with the condition that the recipient work at a public interest job for the summer. She won the fellowship and asked the government agency to allow her to volunteer there. They were thrilled to have her, and she gained valuable experience learning how to prosecute perpetrators of domestic violence. The most important aspect of the job was in her ability to try something out before making a lifetime commitment.

There are wonderful opportunities to be taken advantage of that will help you to see how you feel about a particular area of law before making a long-term commitment. What looks good on television, in a movie, or to another attorney is not necessarily good for you. Even if you just want to try something on for size and it is not what you originally intended to practice, but you are curious about it, go out and see what it is like. You have nothing to lose and everything to gain. Shop around and try on different types of law until the fit feels right.

Gender Benders

Other issues arise that make the practice of law a bit difficult for some people. Sadly, there is an issue of gender discrimination among attorneys. Many female practitioners have expressed disappointment about treatment by their colleagues.

EXHIBIT

A female attorney had experienced gender discrimination right in the courtroom. She was working on a criminal case in a joint defense agreement with a number of other attorneys, all of whom happened to be male. At an administrative hearing, the defense table consisted of six male attorneys and this one lone female. At the prosecution's table, there were a few male United States Attorneys and two male F.B.I. agents. One of the male defense attorneys was attempting to give a presentation to the court. Reacting to the attorney's request for a blackboard or something of that nature to tack a diagram to, the judge turned to the female attorney and said, "Ms. Smith, why don't you hold up the chart for Mr. Jones like one of those girls on the game shows?" Her embarrassment was obvious as she sat there in shock. Luckily in this situation, one of the male attorneys came to her rescue by insisting that they wait for the blackboard.

You may say that you would not have tolerated the judge's remark. However, there are certain professions that have long been male-dominated, and some women feel that they have to put up with more than they should to gain equal footing. It is also fairly well known in the legal community that it can be career suicide for a female to make a complaint against her male employer. Unless you are in a large company where several of your female coworkers have also been harassed or discriminated against, you are going to have a hard time proving your case. The more experience that you have where you have built a good reputation among your colleagues, the easier it will be to find the courage to take a stand against such treatment. If you are working at your first job and you make a claim against someone who has never had a black mark against him, you have a tough decision to make. You know that this is your only reference, and if you go somewhere else for an interview, what will you tell your interviewer? Attorneys are instructed early on that nothing will lose them a job offer faster than to speak harshly of a former employer. You are in a difficult situation. After all of that schooling and all of that tuition, some see it as easier and safer to just move on as though nothing ever happened and hope that your former employer does not say anything bad about you. The real issue becomes whether or not you can live with your decision.

It is awkward to discuss this subject in light of the fact that it is being directed at future attorneys. Our idealistic side tells us that all is going to be right with the world. We think that in the long scheme of life, if anyone should right a wrong or seek justice, it should be an attorney. We are the champions of right, the defenders of all that is good. However, as attorneys, we are even more aware of the implications of bringing a complaint of this nature against someone. We are more in tune with the fact that everything does not always work out the way it should. While lay people often become frustrated when they finally have an experience with the judicial system, attorneys are routinely faced with unfair decisions and a lack of justice and compassion for victims. We know all too well that the odds are not necessarily in our favor.

Some of the discrimination is more subtle.

EXHIBIT

A young female attorney was working for a male solo practitioner. She said that her credentials were impeccable, yet, no matter how hard she tried, and no matter how much responsibility she took on, she was not given the type of salary that her male counterparts received. So, she sat down with her employer to discuss it with him. He asked her what type of salary she felt she deserved. She responded that, considering that she was virtually running both of his offices and traveling between the two of them every other day with no support staff at one of them, she felt that $50,000 was more than fair. With that, her employer laughed and stated, "For $50,000, I'd own you!" It wasn't long before she moved on to another firm for a much higher salary.

Just as there are unhappy women who have had similar experiences to the one above, there are also many wonderful stories about women who have worked their way up in law firms to become partners, or have gone out on their own and have thriving practices. As with everything, there is a down side and there is no reason why you should not be made aware of that here. These are just some of the things worth thinking about and investigating before making the life-altering decision to become an attorney.

Perceptive Blindness

You enter law school feeling as though you have stepped into an environment of success. Everything around you is geared towards being the best, winning the case, beating your adversary, out-arguing your opponent, out-doing your classmates, making law review, being offered a judicial clerkship or a job at the most prestigious firm. You are instructed to dress for success, to stay cool when you are at a loss for words, to be confident and self-assured, and most of all, to be yourself. All signs point to being one of the winners. After all, you have been taught that if you are not a winner, you are nothing more than a loser. However, even those of you who excelled in college are not guaranteed success in law school. You go in like champions and begin your struggle like lost sheep. You do not recognize that much of the harshness of every day law school is for the purpose of shaping the way you think of your future in the legal profession.

You begin to resent the way you think, because you look at things in a much more calculating way, less emotional and more cost-benefit, less creative and more factual. The flip side is that when the facts are not in your favor, you *do* become creative with the law to win your case. You learn the value of using what one attorney referred to as *gray* words, words that stretch the truth or cover it up, as when President Clinton commented that certain conduct did not constitute sexual relations as he understood that term to be defined. Most lay people would take that to mean that he did not even kiss Monica Lewinsky, rather than to think that he was twisting his words to fit the situation. We learn to be vague, to use phrases like—*To the best of my knowledge*. We stretch the truth to manipulate words without getting into trouble. And, we wonder...where do morals and the law diverge from each other? How can something that is immoral not be illegal?

The important thing to remember is that success is measured by how your accomplishments make *you* feel. There is no real yardstick to determine how successful you are because your successes are yours alone and may be thought of as failures to others. You walk through life as an individual. As an attorney, you will strive to beat your opponents, feeling as though that raises you up to a different level. If you are on the losing end, you will feel defeated. Rather than having the perception that being an attorney is a game in which there are winners and losers, you must evolve to a place where you simply try to do your best for your clients, as well as yourself, and to somehow find a resolution that is agreeable to all. It is too strenuous to always feel as though you must prevail. The pressure that comes with that is enormous and makes some lose their way.

You will be endowed with much responsibility, maybe too much at times. You will come to realize that people's lives rest within the realm of your competency and that one small mistake on your part might lead to years of heartache for others. Yet, just as easily, one small victory could bring joy into someone's life in ways that you can never imagine. At times, you will find the court system frustrating and utterly unfair. Clients may badger you; always wanting you to go that extra mile for them; never knowing when enough is enough; thanking you for their victories; and, berating you for their losses. When you combine that with the bad rap that attorneys seem to get all too often, it is easy to understand why some leave the profession altogether and why substance abuse and depression within the legal community has risen to dramatic heights.

Practicing law is a huge burden to bear and not all can carry the weight. That is not to say that all attorneys are stressed-out and depressed. Many are very content in their practices. Many have found ways to take the stress out of their lives. Thankfully, as in many other professions today, there are several lawyer-assistance programs just for that purpose. There is a whole world of help out there for attorneys who suffer from the stress and strain of the profession. All types of seminars, workshops, retreats, and therapy specifically geared towards helping the attorney regain a sense of well-being have popped up. People are meditating, doing yoga, attending conferences, and discussing their feelings. The feedback they receive is enormously helpful, and the most important feature is knowing that there are others out there who feel the same way. There are avenues of relief where attorneys can feel safe enough to reveal their true feelings without thinking they are going to damage their reputations. This is a significant change in the legal community.

Further, just as there are programs to help reduce stress after you enter the legal profession, there are also secrets to surviving the road to joining it. There is the need to get to the root of the discontent and start from there by dispelling the illusions, explaining the realities of every day law practice, and by supplying incoming law students with all of the tools they need to understand and survive what they are about to encounter. There is a harsh reality for those who enter the field unprepared. You must be informed of all of the possibilities before you proceed into law school. The financial cost, the years of stress, the struggle to find your niche, and the pressures of practice all take their toll.

Preconceived notions about an attorney's life, from the comments, the jokes, the media, and the television, are what leads to such confusion and dismay. Not understanding the full gravity of what you are getting involved with can have devastating consequences once you have made such a serious commitment and are left with so much to lose if you walk away. This is your chance to do it right, to enter it fully aware of what to expect, fully primed to face the trials and tribulations, knowledgeable about the ways to conquer adversity, to overcome the doubts and fears, and to walk into it with eyes wide open and minds well prepared!

A Final Thought

At the end of the law school journey, you are in transition. You have survived those three difficult years, as well as the bar exam. You feel a sense of freedom, somewhat akin to what a prisoner of war might feel after being released. A very structured environment became a way of life. Now you leave those hallowed halls, knowing that you are better in many respects. For the moment, you are exhausted. You are a bit weary of your ability to move out into the world and succeed on your own. However, after some deep thought, you will be excited about the future and what you know you are capable of accomplishing as a defender of justice. Walk tall and take pride in how far you have come and how much you have to offer the world. You have truly won your battle and you should be very proud, because it was a long and difficult task!

Index

Author Biography

R. Stephanie Good, Esq., majored in political science at the State University of New York at Stony Brook, where she graduated summa cum laude and was initiated into Phi Beta Kappa. She continued her education at Hofstra University School of Law, where she earned a Juris Doctor degree and held the distinction of being the first recipient of the prestigious David Kadane Public Interest Law Fellowship. In addition, Ms. Good returned to Hofstra Law and earned an LL.M. in International Law. She is licensed to practice law in the State of New York and in the federal courts of the Eastern and Southern Districts of New York, as well.

Ms. Good has practiced law on both private and governmental levels, focusing on environmental law, criminal defense, white collar crime, corporate mergers and acquisitions, estate planning, and entertainment law. She has devoted substantial time to *pro bono* work. She is also a court-appointed special advocate for children in foster care. In addition, she serves as corporate counsel to SilverCreek Entertainment and has co-produced several major news segments for *Extra*, *20/20*, *60 Minutes*, *Good Morning America*, and *Prime-Time Live* in association with SilverCreek Entertainment.

Ms. Good has written several papers involving environmental law, including *International Emissions Trading Schemes*, *Carbon Sinks As Defined in the Kyoto Protocol*, and *Dioxin Contamination in the Indoor Setting*. She is also recognized in several law journals, including the *Kentucky Law Journal* and the *American Political Science Review* for her extensive contributions to research projects involving the confirmation process for United States Supreme Court Justices.